Collaboration for Distance Learning
Information Literacy Instruction

SPEC Kits

Supporting Effective Library Management for Over Twenty Years

Committed to assisting research and academic libraries in the continuous improvement of management systems, OLMS has worked since 1970 to gather and disseminate the best practices for library needs. As part of its committment, OLMS maintains an active publications program best known for its SPEC Kits. Through the OLMS Collaborative Research/Writing Program, librarians work with ARL staff to design SPEC surveys and write publications. Originally established as an information source for ARL member libraries, the SPEC series has grown to serve the needs of the library community worldwide.

What are SPEC Kits?

Published six times per year, SPEC Kits contain the most valuable, up-to-date information on the latest issues of concern to libraries and librarians today. They are the result of a systematic survey of ARL member libraries on a particular topic related to current practice in the field. Each SPEC Kit contains an executive summary of the survey results (previously printed as the SPEC Flyer); survey questions with tallies and selected comments; the best representative documents from survey participants, such as policies, procedures, handbooks, guidelines, websites, records, brochures, and statements; and a selected reading list—both in print and online sources—containing the most current literature available on the topic for further study.

Subscribe to SPEC Kits

Subscribers tell us that the information contained in SPEC Kits is valuable to a variety of users, both inside and outside the library. SPEC Kit purchasers use the documentation found in SPEC Kits as a point of departure for research and problem solving because they lend immediate authority to proposals and set standards for designing programs or writing procedure statements. SPEC Kits also function as an important reference tool for library administrators, staff, students, and professionals in allied disciplines who may not have access to this kind of information.

SPEC Kits can be ordered directly from the ARL Publications Distribution Center. To order, call **(301) 362-8196**, fax **(301) 206-9789**, e-mail **pubs@arl.org**, or go to **http://www.arl.org/pubscat/**.

Information on SPEC Kits and other OLMS products and services can be found on the ARL Web site at **http://www.arl.org/olms/infosvcs.html**. The Web site for the SPEC survey program is **http://www.arl.org/spec/**. The executive summary or flyer for each kit after December 1993 can be accessed free of charge at the SPEC survey Web site.

SPEC Kit 286

Collaboration for Distance Learning
Information Literacy Instruction

July 2005

Association of College and Research Libraries

Distance Learning Section Instruction Committee

Ramona Islam, Chair

Senior Reference and Educational Technology Librarian

Fairfield University

Series Editor: Lee Anne George

SPEC Kits are published by the

Association of Research Libraries
Office of Leadership and Management Services
21 Dupont Circle, NW, Suite 800
Washington, D.C. 20036-1118
(202) 296-2296 Fax (202) 872-0884
http://www.arl.org/olms/infosvcs.html
pubs@arl.org

ISSN 0160 3582

ISBN 1-59407-693-6

EAN 9781594076930

Copyright © 2005

ABOUT THE AUTHORS

This publication was collaboratively authored by members of the Association of College and Research Libraries (ACRL) Distance Learning Section Instruction Committee over a three-year period. In August of 2002, under the chairmanship of Michele Reid, Ramona Islam proposed the idea to distribute a survey tracking collaborative practices in distance library instruction. The committee elected to pursue the project. Communicating via technologies similar to those used for distance learning, members in locations scattered across the United States collectively annotated selected articles and suggested questions for the survey instrument.

In June of 2003, Ramona Islam assumed chairmanship of the committee; shortly thereafter, the first draft of the questionnaire was completed and tested. Darby Syrkin suggested working with the ARL/OLMS SPEC survey program to publish the results. This idea won approval from the committee and Ramona contacted Mary Ellen K. Davis, Executive Director of ACRL, and Lee Anne George, Publications Program Officer at ARL, to negotiate a joint publication contract between ACRL and ARL.

When the committee began working with ARL, members revised the survey instrument in accordance with newer research. ARL distributed the survey in January of 2005. The following spring and summer, committee members compiled the SPEC Kit. Elizabeth Lindsay, Rita Barsun, Mark Horan, and Robert Morrison pored over and selected numerous representative documents submitted by respondents; Patrick Mahoney, Dan H. Lawrence, and Ramona Islam combed through the results in search of correlations; Jonathan Potter, Michele Behr, and Stephanie Buck wrote the executive summary; and Darby Syrkin, Mou Chakraborty, and David Hovde prepared the bibliography. Final editing touches were added by Ramona Islam, Lee Anne George, Kaylyn Hipps of ARL, and the Instruction Committee as a whole.

Full list of authors:

Rita Barsun, Walden University
Michele D. Behr, Western Michigan University
Stefanie Buck, Western Washington University
Marianne Buehler, Rochester Institute of Technology
Mou Chakraborty, Nova Southeastern University
Sharon Elteto, Portland State University
Mark Horan, University of Toledo
David Hovde, Purdue University
Ramona Islam, Fairfield University
Ann G. Jacobson, Naval Postgraduate School
Sharon Hybki Kerr, George Mason University
Dan H. Lawrence, University of Northern Colorado
Elizabeth Lindsay, Washington State University
Robin Lockerby, National University

Cherry Beth Luedtke, Austin Community College
Patrick Mahoney, Central Michigan University
Kate Manuel, New Mexico State University
Mari Miller, University of California-Berkeley
Michelle Millet, Trinity University
Robert Morrison, Utah State University Libraries
Medaline Philbert, Pace University
Jonathan Potter, Eastern Washington University
Michele Reid, McDaniel College
Janie Silveria, California State University, Monterey Bay
Darby Syrkin, Florida State University, Panama City
Patricia Wilson, University of Kentucky
Tommie Wingfield, University of Texas at Arlington

SPEC Kit 286

Collaboration for Distance Learning Information Literacy Instruction

July 2005

SURVEY RESULTS

REPRESENTATIVE DOCUMENTS

Distance Learning Assessment

Position Descriptions

Training Opportunities

SELECTED RESOURCES

SURVEY RESULTS

EXECUTIVE SUMMARY

Introduction

Distance education has become increasingly pervasive in higher education. According to the 2003 EDUCAUSE Center for Applied Research survey on campus support for e-learning courses, 70% of higher education institutions offer distance learning courses online.[1] The 2004 Sloan Center for Online Education report estimates over 2.6 million students enrolled in online courses during the fall of 2004; this represents an increase of 25% since 2002.[2] While a fair number of libraries have offered generous document delivery and reference services to distance learners, fewer have provided ample information literacy instruction. However, progress is being made. Instruction librarians are increasingly reaching out to distance learners and integrating information literacy into their institutions' curricula.

Because the term "distance learning" is popularly used to describe a range of educational endeavors—from on-campus Web-enhanced courses to classes where students and their professors never meet—for the purposes of this survey the authors provided their own definition: a program of study wherein students (distance learners) complete formal coursework off-campus and require library services distinct from those offered to students with ready access to the library building. The term "distance teaching faculty" was defined as instructors, other than librarians, who are teaching a distance learning course, regardless of whether they also are teaching traditional courses on-site. "Information literacy" was defined as a set of skills necessary to locate, critically evaluate, and effectively use information—specifically those skills enumerated in the *Information Literacy Competency Standards for Higher Education*.[3] Finally, "distance information literacy instruction" was defined as any instruction, whether an entire course, a one-shot session, a tutorial, or other effort (except for spontaneous reference interactions or individual reference appointments) that strives to teach one or more information literacy skills to distance learners.

Background

The survey was sent to the 123 ARL member libraries in January 2005. Sixty-nine libraries (56%) responded. The survey asked first if the respondent's institution offered information literacy instruction to off-site students unable to visit the institution's libraries. Forty-three respondents (62%) indicated at least some level of information literacy instruction to off-site students; twenty-six (38%) responded that they didn't offer such services. This is consistent with findings of another survey of ARL libraries that found that 38 of the survey respondents (36.9%) did not provide any library services at all to students at a distance.[4]

Delivery Method

The respondents who do offer information literacy

instruction to off-site students were asked what kinds of delivery methods are being used at their institutions to provide this instruction. The most popular method is asynchronous Internet use, such as tutorials, research guides, e-mail, and discussion lists (40 respondents, or 93%). Next most common is face-to-face library instruction (29, or 67%), though two libraries indicated they had previously done face-to-face instruction but had since dropped it. Twenty-six (60%) of the responding libraries offer synchronous Internet methods including chat, white boards, virtual meeting rooms, and instant messaging. Several libraries also offer instruction through course management systems, such as Blackboard or WebCT. Broadcast media (such as campus television, cable network, and radio announcements) is the least used delivery method; eight libraries currently use it and six others are considering it, but seven have discontinued using it.

Most libraries use a variety of delivery methods. Twenty-three respondents (55%) use three to four different methods; nine (21%) use five to six methods. Asynchronous Internet, face-to-face, and synchronous Internet are the most popular, followed by postal/courier services and teleconferencing. Four institutions rely on a single delivery method: three on asynchronous Internet and one on synchronous Internet.

Collaborative Environment

Collaboration takes place on many levels and with many different departments. When asked if the provision of distance information literacy instruction was a collaborative activity between librarians and other professionals within the institution, 36 (84%) responded "yes." Of these, 35 (97%) have a presence on the institution's main home page. Twenty-six (72%) reported the existence of a strong relationship between the library and a center or unit of the university devoted to improving teaching. Twenty-five (69%) have a presence in the institution's courseware product or portal. Achieving this kind of integral presence in institutional

courseware was later mentioned in comments as one of the strategies proven to facilitate collaboration. Fifteen respondents (44%) indicated that institutional general education requirements were a driving factor in collaborative instructional efforts. Only five (14%) indicated that regional accreditation standards were a driving factor.

Respondents indicated that there are many training opportunities available to librarians, teaching faculty, and other professionals in relevant areas. When asked to list these opportunities, 36 (100%) responded that technology skills training was available to librarians; 34 (94%) said that similar technology training was available to teaching faculty; 32 (89%) that it was available for other professionals. Over 75% of the respondents also reported the availability of training in pedagogy, information literacy skills, and ADA accessibility for librarians. Slightly smaller numbers of respondents reported that these programs were available for teaching faculty and other professionals, as well.

Librarians' service on institutional committees was also mentioned as a factor that facilitates communication and collaboration. All but two respondents (94%) reported that librarians serve on at least one of a number of different types of university committees related to distance learning. Librarian participation is most common on committees concerned with information technology, distance education support, course management software, intellectual property or copyright, and improving teaching.

Collaborative Partners

Twenty-four of the responding libraries (69%) have at least one person responsible for coordinating information literacy instruction for distance learners. While there is no standardization of job titles for the individuals who hold this position, the titles can be divided into those that include "distance learning" and those that don't. Of the total, 15 (63%) have titles that include distance learning. Eight of these are within a department devoted to distance learning. One is within an instructional services department. Four are within a reference department. One is in access services and another is in a branch library.

Nine of the job titles (37%) do not include distance learning, implying that services to distance learners are subsumed in the department or are only a part of the specific librarian's job duties. Four of these are located within or related to instructional services; three are located within a reference department; one is within access services; another is in a branch library.

The reporting structure also does not follow any consistent pattern; 57% report to a director of a department or a department head and 37% report directly to a dean, associate dean, or the university librarian/library director. There is no obvious difference in the reporting structure based on the title held by the individual.

Nineteen of the respondents (53%) indicated that the librarians at their institution have faculty status; eleven (31%) are academic or administrative professionals. Four (11%) indicated an "other" status, which includes academic staff, library faculty, non-regular faculty, and administrative only. Of the librarians responsible for coordinating information literacy for distance learners, 66% have faculty status and 36% do not.

The respondents were asked to estimate the number of individuals with whom they had collaborated to deliver information literacy instruction to distance learners. The responses varied from 2 to 50. The majority of respondents (71%) collaborate with anywhere from 2 to 15 people. The majority of these collaborative efforts involve librarians and teaching (97%), instructional support (57%), academic computing (50%), and instructional design staff (47%). A few respondents collaborate with staff in other units, such as teaching improvement, writing, media, and career centers. All but a handful of the 29 libraries that collaborate with teaching staff report that these staff have a title of faculty or professor; 72% of these have full-time status.

Collaboration takes place primarily with the education (24%), social work (14%), nursing (16%), library and information sciences (8%), and management/business departments (8%). Of the departments named, 12 are in the social sciences, 6 are in the sciences, and 2 are in the humanities. A similar distribution is evident among the faculty who are also distance teaching staff, with 38% in education, 33% in social work, 27% in information science, and 16% each in nursing and engineering.

Collaborative Communication

By far the most popular method used to promote information literacy for distance learners to the teaching faculty is personal contact; this method is followed by Web-based information, local presentations, e-mail, and printed materials. Many libraries apply more than one technique for getting the word out. Four libraries (12%) use between eight and nine communication methods, fourteen (42%) use between five and six, ten use three to four, and the rest use two or fewer. Only one library uses broadcast media (such as campus television, cable network, and radio announcements) and it is among the libraries that use the most communications methods. Only six of the responding libraries (18%) do not actively promote instruction for distance learners.

There does not appear to be a significant difference in the way information literacy instruction is promoted to full-time versus part-time distance teaching faculty. Part-time faculty members are targeted with slightly fewer e-mails—75% vs. 83% for full-time faculty—but slightly more printed promotional materials—87% vs. 77%. Personal contact remains the primary method for promoting information literacy instruction to both full-time and part-time faculty.

Many libraries offer support services to distance learning faculty and staff. The most common include remote or office-based consultations, collection development, copyright compliance, and information alerts about relevant library resources. Other services include attendance at formal presentations of teaching faculty members, needs assessments, and professional development workshops.

Most of these services involve some level of personal contact with faculty. Such types of personal contact are listed in respondents' comments as strategies that have helped facilitate collaboration between librarians and faculty.

Collaborative Teaching

Not surprisingly, the collaborative teaching role for the majority of librarians is either teaching one-shot sessions (88%) or serving as an ad-hoc resource person (65%). Only about 21% of the responding librarians are or have been the primary instructor or the co-instructor for a course. In a few instances, librarians have developed tutorials or acted as consultants. Only two respondents (6%) indicated that their libraries are using synchronous communication, such as chat or monitoring a discussion board, to participate in distance learning courses. Only one library reports librarians participating in all five types of collaborative teaching roles specified on the questionnaire.

Eighty-eight percent of the respondents indicated that a librarian contributes to the content of distance education courses in some form, primarily by providing course-specific research skills content; information literacy skills content; or bibliographies, pathfinders, and other research guides. Librarians also contribute to assignment and syllabus design. A few are responsible for the creation of all course content. Twenty-five of the thirty-four responding libraries (71%) reported that librarians provide both one-shot sessions and course-specific library research skills content.

The teaching role of the respondents who either have the term distance learning in their job title or work within a department devoted to distance learning did not differ significantly from that reported for librarians who did not have the term distance learning in their titles or who did not work within a department devoted to distance learning.

Collaborative Assessment

Educators in all disciplines are increasingly recognizing the importance of assessment in developing effective methods and programs. Therefore it is certainly a cause for concern that only 4 out of the 35 respondents (11%) who answered this section of the survey reported that they conduct any form of assessment to measure whether distance learning students have acquired particular information literacy skills as a result of instruction. Twenty-eight (80%) answered that they don't conduct such assessment; three (9%) answered that they didn't know whether their libraries conduct assessment. Only two of the four libraries that answered "yes" indicated that they conduct that assessment collaboratively with teaching faculty. It is difficult to draw meaningful conclusions from so few responses, so further inquiry into the question of assessment seems merited. What else are these very few libraries doing that exemplifies good practice in distance information literacy instruction? Conducting more in-depth profiles of these institutions might be one avenue of further study.

Although a degree of inconsistency is evident in the numbers of responses to the next three questions in this section of the survey, they further evidence a scarcity of assessment activity in distance information literacy instruction. Only two of seven respondents indicated that information literacy assessment counts toward course grades. In answer to the question on types of assessment methods, only two of six respondents identified assessment methods connected with student projects and only one identified performance-related assessment methods. Only one out of five responding libraries could say that student information literacy skills have improved based on longitudinal comparison of assessment results. It is noteworthy that this library also identified collaboration between librarians and teaching faculty as having contributed to the positive outcome.

Collaborative Challenges and Opportunities

As noted previously, of the many disciplines in which collaborative information literacy instruction occurs, education and social work are high on the list; library and information science, business and management, nursing, and engineering make a strong showing, as well. Within this context, respondents' comments on what has facilitated versus what has hindered collaboration indicate that successful strategies cover a broad range of activities from informal meetings and communications to development of online resources and assignments to establishing subject liaison roles for librarians to conducting face-to-face workshops and orientation sessions. Hindrances include staffing issues, lack of centralization of distance programs, technological roadblocks, and difficulties in communicating with adjunct and off-campus faculty.

In light of these experiences, respondents were asked to identify areas of improvement they plan to implement. Responses included conducting needs assessments, publishing promotional brochures, increasing collaboration with instructional designers, and increasing participation in university-wide formal distance education support groups.

Time and workload issues are among the most common challenges encountered by librarians when attempting to work collaboratively to deliver information literacy instruction to distance learners. Technology and administrative issues also figure prominently. In addition, a number of respondents identified institutional politics, pedagogical issues, and intellectual property issues as challenges. Correlating the responses in this section against the initial section of the survey indicates, as one would expect, that increased collaborative activity results in increased challenges.

The survey concluded by asking for general comments regarding collaboration between librarians and teaching faculty or other individuals to deliver distance information literacy instruction. The following selected comments demonstrate the diverse distance learning environment today.

"Distance programming at our university is not coordinated in any central way, it is very much department-based; there are no campus-wide committees or such to coordinate it. Hence, distance library service generally, and information literacy for distance students in particular, are not a separate function at our library, but are integrated with other services."

"Our institution is not actively involved in distance learning at this time. Only a few courses are offered in the professional schools (social work, nursing, law)."

"We have growing distance learning programs and the libraries are striving to serve them. So far, we've made little progress in the area of information literacy."

"We currently have a position open for a Distance Education librarian. We are expecting this person to take the lead in working collaboratively with academic officials and faculty involved with distance education. This is a new enterprise for us."

"We are really just getting started with trying to forge a connection between librarians and faculty with regard to information literacy, and also getting started with faculty collaboration in distance learning."

Conclusion

The results of this survey underscore the fact that distance learning trends in higher education are in a state of rapid evolution, growth, and uncertainty in relation to traditional on-campus programs. This context of rapid change and uncertain status makes for unique challenges to (and opportunities for) collaborative efforts among librarians, teaching faculty, and others involved in the distance learning process. The large number of survey respondents claiming not to be providing any information literacy instruction at all to distance learners (26 libraries, or 38%) may be disheartening to proponents of distance library services, but it is perhaps not surprising given the uncertain status of distance learning programs that is reflected in respondents' comments about the tendency of these programs to be decentralized, ancillary, and lacking in cohesion with on-campus programs.

On the positive side, many of those libraries that are engaged in distance information literacy instruction appear to be approaching the unique challenges of the distance learning environment dynamically and creatively. Key to the success of these effort has been their collaborations with faculty and other instructional support personnel. As one respondent commented, "Collaboration is clearly important, even critical, to success." And personal contact seems to be the most effective way to facilitate collaboration.

The ability to utilize a variety of tools and technologies, from face-to-face instruction to synchronous and asynchronous online assistance, appears to be a trend for libraries that are taking the lead in distance information literacy instruction. However, the survey reveals that only a very few of these libraries are exploiting to the greatest possible extent recent advances in educational technology, such as e-portfolios, to further librarian involvement in course content creation, teaching, and assessment.

The results of the survey suggest that there are a few truly outstanding distance information literacy programs among ARL libraries and that there are a great many others muddling along as best they can in a challenging and changing environment. This impression is echoed by the literature review and Web site case studies performed by the survey authors, which also point to outstanding programs that deserve further study and emulation as "best practices" models. Among these, North Carolina State, Texas A&M, University of Kansas, and University of Manitoba stand out in terms of promoting collaboration with teaching faculty and instructional designers.

The four libraries that are assessing distance learning students' information literacy skills (Michigan State University, University of Louisville, University of Massachusetts-Amherst, and University of Nebraska-Lincoln) might also be worth examining more closely, particularly Louisville, which attributed evidence of successful distance information literacy instruction to its collaborative efforts with teaching faculty.

In addition to conducting follow-up case studies aimed at highlighting best practices, further useful information could be obtained by repeating the present survey among different sample groups such as smaller non-ARL private and public institutions, community colleges, or even a more cohesive group such as the Association of Jesuit Colleges and Universities, where a shared multi-institutional online distance learning initiative has been developing in recent years. Investigating how the dynamics of collaboration in distance information literacy instruction play out in other higher education environments could shed further light on the conclusions drawn here.

Notes

1. Paul Arabasz and Mary Beth Baker, "ECAR Respondent Summary: Evolving Campus Support Models for E-Learning Courses" (Boulder: EDUCAUSE, 2003), 2, http://www.educause.edu/ir/library/pdf/ERS0303/ekf0303.pdf.
2. I. Elaine Allen and Jeff Seaman, "Entering the Mainstream: The Quality and Extent of Online Education in the United States, 2003 and 2004" (Needham, MA: The Sloan Consortium, 2004), 5, http://www.sloan-c.org/resources/entering_mainstream.pdf.
3. "Information Literacy Competency Standards for Higher Education" (Chicago: American Library Association, 2000), http://www.ala.org/acrl/ilcomstan.html.
4. Zheng Ye (Lan) Yang, "Distance Education Librarians in the U.S.: ARL Libraries and Library Services Provided to Their Distance Users," *The Journal of Academic Librarianship* 31, no. 2 (2005): 92–97.

SURVEY QUESTIONS and RESPONSES

The SPEC survey on Collaboration for Distance Learning Information Literacy Instruction was designed by the members of the ACRL Distance Learning Section Instruction Committee; Ramona L. M. Islam, Chair. These results are based on data submitted by 69 of the 123 ARL member libraries (56%) by the deadline of February 16, 2005. The survey's introductory text and questions are reproduced below, followed by the response data and selected comments from the respondents.

Distance education has become increasingly pervasive in higher education. According to the National Center for Education Statistics, between 1997 and 2001 total enrollments in college level credit-granting distance learning courses more than doubled and the number of post secondary educational institutions offering distance learning courses increased by 68%.[5, 6] In response to survey results from ACRL's 2000 *Academic Library Trends and Statistics*, which focused on the library's role in distance education, Project Coordinator Hugh Thompson concluded that, "Academic libraries will need to cope with potentially explosive growth in distributed learning as an educational model."[7] Recognizing this trend, the *Guidelines for Distance Learning Library Services* call upon librarians to provide equivalent services for all library users, "regardless of where they are located."[8]

While a fair number of libraries have offered generous document delivery and reference services to distance learners, fewer have provided ample information literacy instruction, despite research indicating that library users faced with a proliferation of new technologies require more help than ever developing the skills necessary to locate, critically evaluate, and effectively use information. Progress is being made, however. Increasingly, instruction librarians are reaching out to distance learners and integrating information literacy into their institutions' curricula. Key to the success of this effort has been their collaborations with faculty and other instructional support personnel. For example, librarians at Ball State University have partnered with professors to develop an intensive information literacy course for online nursing students; librarians in the California State University system have offered information literacy instruction to professors via the Web; and librarians in other institutions are working with instructional designers to develop online tutorials and other learning materials for distance learners.

The results of this survey are intended to help librarians promote information literacy among distance learners by identifying effective strategies for collaboration with other professionals in the higher education community. Additionally, it will reveal the extent to which collaboration is a significant factor in the delivery of distance information literacy instruction. The data gathered will track collaborative teaching strategies, challenges and solutions of collaborative projects, assessment of information literacy outcomes in a collaborative distance education environment, promotion of distance information literacy instruction efforts, librarians' involvement on campus distance education committees, and librarians' partners in distance information literacy instruction.

For the purposes of this survey,

Distance learning refers to a program of study wherein students ("distance learners") complete formal coursework off-campus and require library services distinct from those offered to students with ready access to the library building.

Distance teaching faculty refers to instructors, other than librarians, who are teaching a distance learning course, regardless of whether they also are teaching traditional courses on-site.

Information literacy refers to a set of skills necessary to locate, critically evaluate, and effectively use information—specifically those skills enumerated in the *Information Literacy Competency Standards for Higher Education* (see "Standards, Performance Indicators, and Outcomes").

Distance information literacy instruction refers to any instruction, whether an entire course, a one-shot session, a tutorial, or other effort, that strives to teach one or more information literacy skills to distance learners. It does not include spontaneous reference interactions or individual reference appointments.

BACKGROUND

1. Has your library offered information literacy instruction to off-site students who are unable to visit the institution's library? Examples of such instruction include synchronous online sessions, asynchronous Web-based tutorials, learning modules on CD-ROM, librarian visits to a distant learning site, and remote instruction delivered using other learning technologies. Do not include one-on-one reference assistance. (n=69)

Yes	43	62%	Please complete the survey
No	26	38%	Please submit the survey now.

    If yes, please indicate whether your library is using any of the following delivery methods. For methods currently in use, please indicate whether use will continue or be discontinued in the near future. For methods not currently in use, please indicate if the delivery method is being considered for future use, was discontinued in the past five years, or is simply not applicable. Check the best answer for each delivery method. (n=43)

Delivery method	Currently using		Not currently using			Don't know
	continuing	discontinuing	considering	discontinued	N/A	
Asynchronous Internet (Web tutorials, research guides, e-mail, discussion list)	40	—	2	—	1	—
Face-to-face (librarian visits to a distance learning site/ classroom)	29	—	3	2	4	1
Synchronous Internet (chat, white board, virtual meeting room, instant messenger)	26	—	7	2	5	2
Postal/courier services (delivery of print or multimedia instructional materials)	21	2	2	5	9	—
Teleconferencing (videoconferencing, audio conferencing, data conferencing)	12	—	10	4	10	1
Broadcast media (satellite, campus television/cable network, radio)	8	2	6	5	11	3
Other, please specify	5	—	2	—	3	1
Cumulative Responses	42	2	19	11	15	4

Other delivery methods include:

Course management software

Online course (Web CT)

Audio streaming

PowerPoint with voice-over (ViewletCam)

On campus during residential week for MBA students

Web page and face-to-face (students come to the libraries)

2. Is the provision of distance information literacy instruction ever a collaborative activity between librarians and other professionals within the institution, such as teaching faculty, instructional designers, or other individuals? (n=43)

      Yes   36   84%   Please continue.

      No   7   16%   Please skip to question 19.

COLLABORATIVE ENVIRONMENT

3. Which of the following is true for your institution? Check the best answer in each category. (n=36)

	Yes	No	Don't know	N/A
The library has a presence on the home page of the institution's Web site.	35	1	—	—
There is a strong relationship between the library and a center devoted to improving teaching.	26	5	3	1
The library has a presence in the institution's courseware product.	25	9	1	1
The library has a presence in the institution's portal.*	21	5	2	7
Institutional general education requirements were a driving factor for librarian/faculty collaboration.	15	14	5	1
Electronic portfolio software is provided by the institution for use by its members.**	9	11	13	1
Regional accreditation standards were a driving factor for librarian/faculty collaboration.	5	21	8	1
Cumulative Responses	36	31	20	9

* A portal refers to a secure Web site where an institution centralizes information about its members and activities while providing authenticated access to a wide array of Web-based services and resources.

** Electronic portfolio software allows individuals to electronically warehouse examples of their work from any project or course for their personal assessment of development or assessment by others.

4. Which of the following opportunities are available to librarians, teaching faculty, and other professionals at your institution? Check the best answer in each category. (n=36)

Y = Opportunity is available N = Opportunity is not available ? = Don't know N/A = Not applicable	Librarians N=36				Teaching Faculty N=34				Other Professionals N=33			
	Y	N	?	N/A	Y	N	?	N/A	Y	N	?	N/A
Technology skills training	36	—	—	—	34	—	—	—	32	—	—	—
Teacher training (pedagogy)	29	1	5	—	32	—	2	—	19	1	11	—
Information literacy skills training	28	5	2	1	24	6	3	—	21	4	7	1
ADA/accessibility skills training	27	4	4	1	20	2	11	1	21	2	8	1
Flexible work schedules to accommodate teaching in multiple time zones or after hours	26	3	5	2	21	—	11	1	8	—	24	1
Financial compensation for extra teaching, collaboration, or instructional design duties	10	18	4	3	16	3	13	—	5	3	24	—
Cumulative Responses	36	21	15	6	34	9	23	2	33	6	29	3

5. On what institution-wide committees related to distance learning do librarians participate? Check all that apply. (n=35)

Information technology committee	23	66%
Distance education support committee	20	57%
Course management software committee	16	46%
Intellectual property/copyright committee	16	46%
A center devoted to improving teaching	16	46%
Curriculum planning committee	11	31%
ADA awareness/accessibility committee	11	31%
Instructional design committee	6	17%
Librarians do not participate on such committees	2	6%
Other, please specify	15	43%

Other committees include:

Information Literacy Committee

General Education Council

Unified Service Working Group to offer seamless distributed learning services

Senate Committee on Open Learning

E-course Working Group

Campus Writing Board

Distance Education Users Group (Looks at technology, instruction, communication needs. Members are faculty and staff from across the university.)

Advisory Board for Learning in a Technology-Rich Environment Quality Enhancement Plan

Quarterly meeting with Lifelong Learning staff and Director

University Outreach Council

Continuous Education Coordinating Council

Academic Integrity Committee/University Honor Council

COLLABORATIVE PARTNERS

6. Is there a professional in your library who is responsible for coordinating information literacy instruction for distance learners? If so, please provide the individual's job title, their department, and the title of the position(s) to which they report. (n=35)

Yes	24	69%
No	11	31%

Title specifies distance learning; within a department devoted to Distance Learning		
Job Title:	Department:	Reports to:
Outreach & Distance Education Librarian	Outreach & Distance Education	Associate Dean of Libraries
Coordinator of Library Services for Distance Education	Distance Education	Director of Research and Information Services
Distance Learning Librarian	Distance Learning Library Services	Head, Access and Delivery
Coordinator, Distance Learning Library Services	Distance Learning Library Services	Director
Coordinator	Library Distance Learning Services	Associate Director for Public Services
Distance Education Coordinator	Office of Distance Education and Undergraduate Services	Associate Dean
Instruction Librarian, Distance Learning Services	Distance Learning Services	Head, Distance Learning Services
Off-Campus Librarian	Libraries	Head, Elizabeth Dafoe Library

Title specifies distance learning; within Instructional Services		
Job Title:	Department:	Reports to:
Coordinator for Distance Learning Information Services	Instructional Services	Head of Instructional Services

Title specifies distance learning; within Reference		
Job Title:	Department:	Reports to:
Outreach Librarian	Information Services	Head, Information Services
Distributed Learning Services Librarian	General Information Services	Assistant University Librarian for Public Services
Distributed Education Library Services Coordinator	Reference Department	Head, Reference Department
Distance Education and Outreach Services Librarian	Reference	Head, Reference and Instructional Services

Title specifies distance learning; within Access Services		
Job Title:	Department:	Reports to:
Distance Learning Librarian	Direct Services	Director of Direct Services

Title specifies distance learning; within other department		
Job Title:	**Department:**	**Reports to:**
Director of Library Services, School of Continuing and Professional Studies	Clemons Library (not affiliated with School of Cont & Prof Studies)	Director of Clemons Library

Title does not specify distance learning; within Instructional Services		
Job Title:	**Department:**	**Reports to:**
Coordinator of Instructional Services	Library Administration	Associate University Librarian for Public Services
Coordinator for Information Literacy Services and Instruction	Administration	Associate University Librarian for Services
Head of Instructional Programs	Instructional Programs, University Libraries	Associate Dean
Instruction Coordinator	New Brunswick Libraries	Director, New Brunswick Libraries

Title does not specify distance learning; within Reference		
Job Title:	**Department:**	**Reports to:**
Reference Librarian	Reference	Head, of Reference Department
Head, Research and Instructional Services	Research and Instructional Services	Head, Research and Instructional Services
Reference & Instruction	Reference	Head, Reference & Instruction

Title does not specify distance learning; within Access Services		
Job Title:	**Department:**	**Reports to:**
Head, Access Services	Public Services	Associate Dean for Public Services

Title does not specify distance learning; within other department		
Job Title:	**Department:**	**Reports to:**
Head Librarian	Social Work Library	Associate University Librarian for Public Services

7. What is the status of librarians at your institution? (n=36)

Faculty   19   53%

Academic/Administrative Professional   11   31%

Mixture of Faculty and
    Academic/Administrative Professional   2   5%

Classified Staff   —   —

Other, please describe   4   11%

Other status includes:

Academic Staff

Library Faculty

Non-Regular Faculty

Administrative only

8. With approximately how many individuals have librarians collaborated in the past calendar year to deliver information literacy instruction to distance learners? (n=24)

Minimum	Maximum	Mean	Median	Std Deviation
2	50	15.5	12.0	14.4

# of Individuals	2	3	4	5	6	8	12	15	20	25	36	41	45	50
# of Responses	2	2	3	1	2	1	2	4	1	2	1	1	1	2

With what types of professional staff outside of the library have librarians collaborated to deliver information literacy instruction to distance learners? Please check all that apply and specify the job title and department for up to 3 individuals in each category. (n=30)

Teaching staff	29	97%
Instructional support staff	17	57%
Academic computing staff	15	50%
Instructional design staff	14	47%
Center for improving teaching staff	8	27%
Writing Center staff	7	23%
Media Center staff	4	13%
Career Center staff	1	3%
Language Resource Center staff	—	—
ADA/accessibility support staff	3	10%
Other staff, please specify	5	17%

Other staff include:

Desktop Coaching Staff

Copyright

Continuous Education and Outreach Staff

Administrative Support Staff

Teaching Staff Job Titles

Professor	25
Faculty	19
Associate Professor	5
Instructor	4
Assistant Professor	3
Project director	2
Adjunct	2
Associate Dean	1
Coordinator of Distance Learning	1

Teaching Staff Departments

Education (15)

Social Work (9)

Nursing (6)

Library and Information Science (5)

Management/Business (5)

Engineering (3)

English (3)

Criminal Justice (2)

Political Science (2)

Psychology (2)

Aboriginal Focus Program

Agriculture

Architecture

Computer Science

Human Environmental Science

Institute on Aging

Leadership & Lifelong Learning

Rehabilitation Science

Spanish

Study Abroad

Theater

Instructional Support Staff Job Titles

Program Manager/Administrator/Coordinator (5)

Associate Director for Academic Programs and Services

Associate Director, Learning Technology Service

Coordinator of Student Services

Director of Testing Services

Educational Programmers

Instructional Designer

Instructional Support Specialist

Managing Director of Executive Doctorate of Management

Program Development Specialist for Distance Learning

Senior Continuing Education Coordinator

Technology Consultant

Web Content Developer

Instructional Support Staff Departments

Aboriginal Focus Program

Center of Instructional Design

Continuing Education Centers

Department of Health

Distance Education and Learning Technology Applications

Distance Learning Programs

Education Media Services

Independent and Distance Learning

Information Sciences

MU Direct

Public Administration

School of Management

Social Welfare

Teaching & Academic Support Center

Transuniversity

Teaching & Leadership

University Outreach

Academic Computing Staff Job Titles

Assistant Director, Academic Technology

Blackboard Portfolio Manager

Blackboard Specialist

Director of Information Systems

Education Support Technologist

Educational Technology Coordinator

IT Security Manager

Instructional Designer

Instructional Toolkit Consultant

Senior Designer Instructional Technologies

Senior Systems Specialist

Academic Computing Staff Departments

Academic Computing and Network Services

Center for Instructional Technology

Educational Technologies

Engineering

Information Technology

Instructional Technology Services

Office of Library Technology

Teaching and Learning Technology

Instructional Design Staff Job Titles

Instructional Designer (6)

Educational Programs Specialist

Educational Technology Coordinator

Instructional Design Architect

Lecturer, Educational Technologies

Manager of Faculty Development

Media Coordinator

Virtual University Developers

Instructional Design Staff Departments

Center for Instructional Design

Distance Education and Learning Technology Applications

Educational Technologies

Extended Education and Outreach

Instructional Development & Support

Instructional Technology Services

Teaching and Learning Technology

Transuniversity

World Campus

Center for Improving Teaching Staff Job Titles

Administrative Assistant

Assistant Director

Assistant to Provost

Coordinator of Teaching Technologies

Director, Instructional Development

Instructional Technology Consultant

Professor

Program Coordinator

Center for Improving Teaching Staff Departments

Center for Teaching and Learning

Center for Teaching Excellence

Delphi Center

Economics/Libraries, Computing, Technology

Program for Excellence in Teaching

Writing Center Staff Job Titles

Administrative Specialist

Assistant Director of the Writing Program

Director

Program Manager

Writing Center Staff Departments

Campus Writing Center

College of Arts and Sciences

Writing Center

Writing Program

Media Center Staff Job Titles

Director

Multimedia Consultant

Professor

Senior Software and Faculty Support

Media Center Staff Departments

Academic Support Center

Center for Instructional Technology

Media and Current Periodicals

Office of Information Technologies

ADA/Accessibility Support Staff Titles

Accessibility Specialist

Director

ADA/Accessibility Support Staff Departments

Access Office

Center for Instructional Technology

Career Center Staff Job Title

Director, Faculty & Staff Career Services

Career Center Staff Department

University Human Resources

Other Staff Job Titles

Administrative Support Staff

Associate Vice President for Outreach

Continuous Education and Outreach Staff

Desktop Coaching Staff

Endowed Chair for Scholarly Communication

Other Staff Departments

Agricultural Extension

College of Medicine

Copyright Clearing Center

Instructional Services

University Libraries

University Outreach

Of the individuals listed above who are also distance teaching faculty, please indicate how many hold each particular academic status. (n=25)

Full-time	18	72%
Part-time or adjunct	8	32%
Other, please specify:	2	8%
Don't know	7	28%

Other statuses include:

Lecturer

Classified staff and non-tenured faculty

COLLABORATIVE COMMUNICATION

9. How does your library promote information literacy instruction for distance learners to the teaching faculty and other concerned professionals? Check all that apply. (n=34)

Personal contact (in-person meetings, telephone conversations, conference calls)	32	94%
Web-based information ("what's new," FAQ)	25	74%
Local presentations (participation at seminars, workshops, formal meetings)	22	65%
E-mail (announcements, discussion list)	21	62%
Printed promotional materials (letters, handouts, newsletters, brochures)	20	59%
Professional presentations (participation at academic conferences attended by teaching faculty and other professionals serving distance learners)	11	32%
Research studies (publication in academic journals, purposeful distribution of relevant articles)	7	21%
Promotional giveaways (mugs, mouse pads, pens, bookmarks)	6	18%
Broadcast media (campus television/cable network, radio announcements)	1	3%
The library does not actively promote information literacy instruction for distance learners to the specified individuals.	6	18%
Other, please specify	5	15%

Other promotion techniques include:

Regular attendance, reports, and submissions to Continuing Education faculty council

Library-sponsored symposia

Blackboard

Course Management System

10. Aside from instructional services provided directly to students in a particular distance learning course, and regardless of any promotional implications, what services or perks do librarians at your institution offer in support of the distance teaching faculty and other professionals serving distance learners? Check all that apply. (n=35)

Remote or office-based consultations	27	77%
Collection development	24	69%
Copyright compliance	19	54%
Informational alerts about relevant library resources	19	54%
Attendance at formal presentations of teaching faculty members or other professionals serving distance learners	18	51%
Needs assessment(s) to discover the needs of teaching faculty members and other professionals serving distance learners	14	40%
ADA/accessibility compliance	13	37%
Professional development workshops (plagiarism prevention, copyright, instructional design)	13	37%
Informal business outings (e.g., meetings over coffee or lunch)	13	37%
Congratulatory notes recognizing accomplishments of teaching faculty members or other professionals serving distance learners	7	20%
Blog or discussion list	5	14%
Other, please specify	4	11%

Other services include:

Assistance with developing course management sites and electronic reserves

Home page tailored to students' specific needs

Web and van delivery of library materials; online requesting; e-reserves; online reference; media materials

COLLABORATIVE TEACHING

11. In what role have librarians participated in the **teaching** of distance learning courses, including library courses and any other type of course, at your institution? Check all that apply. (n=34)

One-shot session instructor/guest lecturer	30	88%
Ad-hoc resource person	22	65%
Primary instructor of course	7	21%
Co-instructor (team teacher)	7	21%
Librarians have not participated in the teaching of distance learning courses	3	9%
Other, please specify	6	18%

Other roles include:

Development of course-specific tutorials on use of library resources and technology

Consultant

Chat and e-mail reference support; creating course related Web pages

Monitor discussion board in LMS throughout duration of course

Instructional design librarian, instruction in teaching with technology

Advisory; develop bibliographies and handouts

12. What contributions have librarians made to the **content** of distance learning courses, including library courses and any other type of course, at your institution? Check all that apply. (n=34)

Course-specific library research skills content	30	88%
Provision of bibliographies, pathfinders, or library research guides	28	82%
Information literacy skills content	23	68%
Assignment design	13	38%
Syllabi creation	6	18%
Creation of all (or most) course content	3	9%

Librarians have not contributed to the content of distance learning courses.	1	3%
Other, please specify	6	18%

Other contributions include:

Respond to specific info needs

Consultation

Assessment of collection's ability to support new courses

A Web site for course materials

Tutorial

Promote library resources; provide reference service

COLLABORATIVE ASSESSMENT

13. Do librarians at your institution conduct any form of assessment to measure whether distance learning students have acquired particular information literacy skills as a result of instruction? Check the best answer. (n=35)

Yes	4	11%	Please continue.
No	28	80%	Please skip to question 18.
Don't know	3	9%	Please skip to question 18.

If yes, do librarians conduct such assessment in conjunction with teaching faculty? Check the best answer. (n=4)

Yes	2	50%
No	1	25%
Don't know	1	25%

14. Is the performance of distance learning students on information literacy assessments generally considered toward their overall course grades? Check the best answer. (n=7)

Yes	2	29%
No	3	42%
Don't know	2	29%

15. What methods are used to assess whether or not distance learning students have acquired particular information literacy skills as a result of instruction? Check all that apply. (n=6)

Teaching faculty feedback (quality of sources consulted in students' research papers, etc.)	5	83%
Student feedback (survey questionnaire, focus group, rating scale)	3	50%
Student projects (research journal, prospectus, process log, annotated bibliography)	2	33%
Student performance (exam, quiz, exercises)	1	17%
Other, please specify	1	17%
No assessment has been done.		

16. What does the library's latest assessment of distance learning students' information literacy skills reveal? Check the best answer. (n=5)

Students' information literacy skills have improved overall	1	20%
Students' information literacy skills have worsened overall	—	—
Overall, students' information literacy skills have neither improved nor worsened	—	—
No comparison data exists from prior years	2	40%
The library has not compiled and analyzed the results of assessments	2	40%

17. Concerning your answer to the above question, which is true? Check the best answer. (n=2)

Collaboration between librarians, teaching faculty, and/or other professionals appears to have contributed to this outcome	1	50%
Lack of collaboration between librarians, teaching faculty, and/or other professionals appears to have contributed to this outcome	—	—
Collaboration or the lack thereof between librarians, teaching faculty, and/or other professionals appears to be unrelated to this outcome	—	—
Librarians have not determined whether collaboration or the lack thereof between librarians, teaching faculty, and/or other professionals is related to this outcome	1	50%

COLLABORATIVE CHALLENGES AND OPPORTUNITIES

18. Concerning the library's involvement in the collaborative delivery of information literacy instruction to distance learners, please specify the following. (n=33)

Academic Disciplines Involved (n=33)

Education (17)

Social Work (11)

Library and Information Science (8)

Business and Management (7)

Nursing (6)

Engineering (5)

English (2)

Foreign Languages (2)

Social Sciences (2)

Aboriginal Focus Program

Agriculture

Architecture

Art

Continuing Education

Criminal Justice

Entomology

Health Sciences

Humanities

Kinesiology

Law

Music

Nutrition

Pharmacy

Public Health

Recreation and Park Administration

Selected Comments from Respondents

Strategies Employed That Have Facilitated Collaboration (n=26)

"Assignments appropriate to resources available"

"Assistance with copyright issues"

"Asynchronous instruction"

"Attending faculty meetings and meetings with distance education faculty"

"Collaborating on assignment development"

"Collaborating on integration of library resources into course page"

"Collaborating on the design of Web-based tutorials"

"Connection with Academic Computing. They specifically work with faculty on integrating technology into their coursework. Librarians and Academic Computing staff now work in pairs to deliver workshops to faculty (technology and information literacy integration workshops)."

"Departmental workshops to faculty demonstrating existing examples. This gives faculty an idea of what type of collaboration is possible and the value."

"Established subject liaison roles of librarians"

"Faculty actively requiring students participation"

"Frequent e-mail communications"

"Going to continuing education social events"

"Having central unit send out library brochures to all distance learners enrolled in College of Continuing Education."

"Informal meetings with individual professors"

"Involvement with university technical support group for virtual courses"

"Joint Teaching"

"Librarian creating Web site for a specific DE class"

"Librarian offering information literacy instruction to a distance class over statewide television"

"Librarians participating in on- and off-campus orientations for new students in distance programs"

"Librarians working with faculty in the development of online library instruction tutorials"

"Library faculty working with instructional designers for distance faculty's courses"

"Providing online research guides and tutorials and access to materials"

"Previously established close working relationship between librarians and School of Management"

"Support of the Dean and the School; direct contact with individual faculty members"

"Visiting the remote campus in person to provide instruction"

"Volunteering to create online course guides and subject research guides for classes based on current syllabus"

"Working with instructional designers"

Strategies Employed That Have Hindered Collaboration (n=10)

"Adjunct faculty do not always get the same information"

"Decentralized campus administration"

"Delivery of materials not available electronically"

"Departmental cultures that prefer to 'go it alone'"

"Faculty see no difference between in-class and remote presentation of media"

"Lack of centralization of distance education programs"

"Lack of collaborative technology for instruction"

"Lack of response by faculty to outreach."

"Lack of shared software and other technologies"

"Lack of staff and software to develop information literacy modules for Web-based courses"

"Many faculty are not expert enough in developing the technology needed to assist distance learners. When librarians work with them the faculty many times want the librarian to do all the technical work (Web page development, course management assistance.) Luckily we can refer them to academic computing for this type of training."

"The amount of time it takes to develop many online resources cuts into the amount of faculty we can assist with this. So, we have found we can only collaborate with a few faculty a semester if it is this intense."

Improvements Librarians Plan to Implement (n=17)

"About to conduct needs assessment of faculty and students"

"About to publish promotional brochure"

"Assessment tests for Information Literacy Skills"

"Continued networking with faculty"

"Dedicate more staff time to distance learning"

"Encourage instructors to allow librarian participation in their course discussion boards"

"Greater outreach to distance education faculty"

"Increased collaboration with instructional designers"

"Information literacy modules for Web courses"

"Make recommendations on more effective assignments"

"More aggressive marketing through liaison librarians"

"More communication with departments delivering courses electronically"

"More integration into course management system of subject-related information literacy/library resources"

"More librarians presenting at faculty sessions"

"Participating in university-wide formal distance education support groups"

"Student and faculty feedback on library instruction"

"Update Web site in consultation with faculty and students"

"Videostreaming"

"Working with our staff from the Campus Media Center: upload videos of instructional sessions that can be viewed online. Have the technology—waiting for the streaming server to be up and running."

19. What are the **three** most challenging issues librarians have encountered when attempting to work collaboratively to deliver information literacy instruction to distance learners? Please check up to THREE. (n=40)

Time/workload issues	26	65%
Technology issues	16	40%
Administrative issues	11	28%
Institutional political issues	9	23%
Pedagogical issues	7	18%
Intellectual property issues	6	15%
Financial issues	3	8%
Librarians have not attempted to work collaboratively for this purpose	3	8%
Librarians have not encountered significant challenges in this effort	2	5%
ADA accessibility issues	—	—
Foreign language issues	—	—
Other, please specify	11	28%

Selected Comments from Respondents

Time/Workload

"Trying to track down faculty to let them know about services"

"Time to learn technology and course content of primary concern"

"Extremely time consuming developing the online resources, not to mention teaching via a platform such as Web CT (follow up needed etc.)"

Technology

"Variety of technologies used and bandwidth issues"

"Compatibility issues with technology. Have to go to the least common denominator. Spent a lot of time on chat and e-mail working through technology issues for various segments of Web CT."

Administrative

"Highly decentralized"

"Registration of students on multiple campuses"

Institutional Politics

"There is no office for Distance Education in this campus; therefore, no coordination."

"[The university] has yet to develop clear policies concerning distance education, distributed education, and Web-centered education. In the absence of clear commitments, we make plans for more detailed and systematic response to distance learners."

Pedagogy

"Few research assignments made to distance learning classes."

"Just beginning to see (since I'm on instructional technology task force at the campus) just how unsound a lot of their pedagogical approaches are when developing online teaching resources."

Intellectual Property

"TEACH Act implications for use of media in class"

"License agreements"

Other

"I wonder if faculty see this as a true need, or as important."

"Invisibility of distance learning: distance learning faculty are often either adjuncts or are part of a regular department."

"Institutional support for consistent technological applications; financial, training, and equipment."

"Many distance education courses are designed not to require library research. This makes it difficult for many instructors to see collaborative possibilities."

"Distance ed is not centralized."

"Faculty do not really want to make room in the syllabus for it, so have to catch new faculty or new class or class in process of being redesigned."

"No university-wide credit course for information literacy instruction"

"Many adjunct faculty are temp employees and are not entered into the university system until they receive their 1st paycheck halfway thru the semester; i.e. there is no contact info online for them."

ADDITIONAL COMMENTS

20. Please enter any additional information regarding collaboration between librarians and teaching faculty or other individuals to deliver distance information literacy instruction that may assist the authors in accurately analyzing the results of this survey.

Selected Comments from Respondents

"Distance programming at our university is not coordinated in any central way, it is very much department-based; there are no campus-wide committees or such to coordinate it. Hence, distance library service generally, and information literacy for distance students in particular, are not a separate function at our library, but are integrated with other services. As well, although information literacy is a strong element of library service generally, we do not have an information literacy program that is aimed at distance learners per se. The information literacy training available to distance students consists of two things: the Web-based tutorials that are available to any student regardless of location; and course-specific instruction that would be set up for a specific course, by the liaison librarian for the department working in conjunction with the faculty member involved, and in some cases other personnel such as departmental admin assistant staff. Only occasionally have librarians worked directly with instructional designers."

"Our institution is not actively involved in distance learning at this time. Only a few courses are offered in the professional schools (social work, nursing, law)."

"[The] university has a decentralized system and it has a very small distance learning program. There is not a common support structure for distance learners. We do not maintain library-wide statistics or information on distance learner support issues."

"We have growing distance learning programs, and the libraries are striving to serve them. So far, we've made little progress in the area of information literacy. We were invited to talk with both faculty and students in a new agricultural education DL program. We have many DL programs in academic disciplines served by the health sciences library. Librarians there have been effective in developing tutorials to serve these programs."

"We currently have a position open for a Distance Education librarian. We are expecting this person to take the lead in working collaboratively with academic officials and faculty involved with distance education. This is a new enterprise for us."

"We are really just getting started with trying to forge a connection between librarians and faculty with regard to information literacy, and also getting started with faculty collaboration in distance learning. Progress is slow due to work load constraints as well as either indifference or education politics issues between librarians and faculty. Some faculty are open to information literacy collaboration whereas others see it as an intrusion."

"[This university] bought a tutorial from another university and proceeded to adapt the tutorial to its needs and to focus on its local characteristics. The Library Instruction Coordinator has worked to adapt the tutorial but didn't collaborate with faculties."

"Although our institution promotes many online courses, there are few faculty that have done this well. Much might stem from not having sufficient training in technology, perhaps the time element and some from not understanding that they need to adjust the way they present information in an online arena. Librarians have been making good progress in connecting with faculty to incorporate information literacy into their online work—partly thanks to our collaborations with the staff from Academic Computing.

I was able to produce two 3 credit Web CT courses on information literacy for several subject areas (in collaboration with faculty) and a couple of other librarians are working steadily with distance ed faculty to integrate info lit into online portals/ Web CT/Web pages. A few librarians teach classes at remote locations (one shots and full courses). We are not required to do any of this for promotion and we do not get tenure. So, librarians here are motivated to go the extra mile because of connections with faculty and students.

We have been working with the Office of Information Technology to provide access to all students (distance or not) to our online databases. Until this year, many distance students were not authenticated to use them. So, our collaborative efforts should increase now that more distance students can actually get into the databases we're trying to promote."

"Collaboration is clearly important, even critical, to success in the continuing ed environment."

Notes

5. Laurie Lewis et al., *Distance Education at Postsecondary Education Institutions: 1997–98*, NCES 2000-013 (Washington, D.C.: U.S. Department of Education, National Center for Education Statistics, 1999), http://nces.ed.gov/pubs2000/2000013.pdf.

6. Tiffany Waits et al., *Distance Education at Degree-Granting Postsecondary Institutions: 2000–2001*, NCES 2003-017 (Washington, D.C.: U.S. Department of Education, National Center for Education Statistics, 2003), http://nces.ed.gov/pubs2003/2003017.pdf.

7. Hugh Thompson, "The Library's Role in Distance Education: Survey Results from ACRL's 2000 Academic Library Trends and Statistics," *C&RL News* 63, no. 5 (2002), http://www.ala.org/ala/acrl/acrlpubs/crlnews/backissues2002/may/librarysrole.htm.

8. "Guidelines for Distance Learning Library Services" (Chicago: American Library Association, 2005), http://www.ala.org/acrl/resjune02.html.

All URLs accessed July 1, 2005.

RESPONDING INSTITUTIONS

University of Alabama
University at Albany, SUNY
University of Alberta
University of Arizona
Arizona State University
Auburn University
Boston College
Brigham Young University
University of British Columbia
University at Buffalo, SUNY
University of California, Davis
University of California, Riverside
University of California, San Diego
University of California, Santa Barbara
Canada Institute for Scientific and Technical
   Information
Case Western Reserve University
University of Chicago
Cornell University
University of Florida
George Washington University
University of Georgia
University of Guelph
University of Houston
University of Illinois at Urbana-Champaign
Indiana University Bloomington
University of Iowa
Iowa State University
University of Kansas
Kent State University
University of Kentucky
Université Laval
Library and Archives Canada
Library of Congress
University of Louisville

McGill University
McMaster University
University of Manitoba
University of Massachusetts, Amherst
Massachusetts Institute of Technology
University of Miami
University of Michigan
Michigan State University
University of Minnesota
University of Missouri
Université de Montréal
National Library of Medicine
University of Nebraska–Lincoln
University of North Carolina at Chapel Hill
North Carolina State University
Ohio University
University of Oregon
University of Pennsylvania
Pennsylvania State University
University of Pittsburgh
Rice University
Rutgers University
Smithsonian Institution
University of Southern California
Southern Illinois University Carbondale
Syracuse University
University of Tennessee
University of Texas at Austin
Texas A&M University
Vanderbilt University
University of Virginia
Washington State University
Washington University in St. Louis
Wayne State University
University of Western Ontario

REPRESENTATIVE DOCUMENTS

Publicizing the Service

The University of Georgia Libraries   home   sitemap   search

home > reference > distance learning

Distance Learning

Goal

- The goal of the UGA Libraries' Distance Learning Service is to ensure that distance learners at UGA have access to library services equivalent to on-campus students. This includes students registered in both off-campus and online UGA courses. As part of this mission, we also provide service to UGA faculty and staff living or working outside of the Athens area.

Getting started

- Connecting to GALILEO Databases from off-campus.

-
  Obtaining a UGA Library account.

Electronic Reserves

- Electronic Reserves provide access to materials instructors have made available to your class.

Obtaining books and articles

- Books - Information on obtaining books using GIL, the UGA Libraries catalog, as well as the University System of Georgia's Universal Borrowing program and NetLibrary, a collection of over 30,000 electronic books.

- Articles- GALILEO is a portal of over 300 library subscribed databases available to the UGA community. GALILEO contains article citations and abstracts, full-text journal, magazine and newspaper articles, and other resources of interest to researchers. You can locate full-text journals and magazines using the Electronic Journal Locator and Find It.

- Electronic Reserves are materials instructors have made available to your class.

Research Help

- Tutorials - Librarians have created numerous tutorials to make using our

Reference

Department

Research Central
Ask A Question
Classes and

Conferences
Disability Services
Distance Learning
Hours
How to Reach Us
Staff

resources easier.

- <u>Research guides</u> - Research Central is a starting point to begin researching a topic beginning provides subject specific research help.

- <u>Help for Distance Learners</u> - Contact a librarian by telephone, email or on-line chat.

- In person - If you have the opportunity to travel to Athens, we welcome the opportunity to help you face to face. Please see the UGA Libraries <u>Hours</u> and <u>Directions</u> beforehand.

Faculty Services

- <u>Reserve Materials List</u> - Faculty should use this form to place an item on Electronic Reserve for your class.

Distance Learning links

- <u>Links</u> to resources for UGA and USG Distance Learning students, including specific programs, affiliated libraries and computing resources.

(877) 314-5560 Toll Free | <u>Email</u> | Fax (706) 583-0268

 Last Updated:5/11/2005

Library » services for » distance students

Library services for distance education students and open learners

Library card

Open learners receive their library card from the <u>Office of Open Learning</u> and are registered automatically on the library's system. Open learners registered in general interest courses, certificate programs, or continuing education courses can apply for a <u>community borrower </u>card. A $20.00 fee applies. *Restricted privileges apply.*

Distance education students and open learners registered in a degree course with a valid UoG (University of Guelph) <u>photo ID card</u> or a library card can access library resources 24-7 from home and can use our courier service. Start by <u>logging on</u>. **Having trouble logging on?**

To use other university libraries yourself

<u>Canadian University Reciprocal Borrowing Agreement</u> - borrow directly from most Canadian university libraries with your valid UoG photo ID card.

<u>Other university library catalogues</u> - *University of Toronto and OCAD do not extend reciprocal borrowing privileges to undergraduate students.*

To search for items available electronically

Many journal articles and books are available electronically.
<u>Electronic books</u> - search TRELLIS for electronic books.
<u>Journal indexes</u> - search for articles on a topic use the journal indexes. For help on choosing which databases to use see <u>Subject and course guides</u>. For articles without direct electronic links search for the journal title in <u>TRELLIS</u> or the <u>Electronic Journals page</u>.

To use our courier service ... what you need to know

Please note : Distance and open learners that reside within a reasonable distance of Guelph are **not** eligible to use our courier service.

- A street address and phone number is required for delivery.
- Deliveries are made Monday to Friday from 9 am to 5 pm.
- Our courier service requires a signature upon delivery.
- Delivery to a place of work is acceptable. Please be sure of the correct address.
- Our courier service will not deliver to a post office box.
- Allow for as much lead time as possible.
- Delivery is generally within 2-3 business days.

To get a TRELLIS item delivered to you

- **Books** - request a <u>hold/recall</u>. When you select a **pick-up location** you must select **GuelphDistEd Circ**
- You will be notified by email when the item is available. We will retrieve, charge out, and send the item to you via courier.

To get an article delivered to you

- Send us an <u>email</u> and we will retrieve, photocopy, and send the item to you via courier. *<u>Copyright</u> restrictions apply*
- When ordering a journal article by email include the full citation: author, article title, journal title, volume, issue and page numbers required. Include the journal title call number.

DO NOT choose TUGdoc to have a UoG article delivered to you

To get an article from WLU, WU or the Annex delivered to you

- Once you find the journal title in TRELLIS select *Request item from TRELLIS* and then *Request **TUGdoc***. When you select a pick-up location under 'Tell us where to send the article' choose:

Off campus, for Guelph distance education students

Under Special instructions add **:**

Attention : Doug Morrison, UG Library Learning Commons

- Allow **at least** 5 business days.

To order an interlibrary loan yourself use RACER

RACER lets you search and request items from other Ontario university libraries. Enter your *14-digit library barcode as the login* and *your surname, in lower case, as the password*. If you do not find the item you're seeking, complete a blank request form in RACER by clicking Requests, then Create . Library staff will search outside Ontario for the item. Allow **at least** 15 business days.

Need further assistance?

Email us at libde@uoguelph.ca. We can advise you about what to search and how to do a search. We will also troubleshoot if you are having difficulty using TRELLIS or the journal indexes but good online help is available via each database help screen. Try our **tutorials** or **research help** pages.

IUB Libraries

IUCAT/Databases

IUB home

Ask a librarian

Site Search

IUB Libraries
Distributed
Education
Services
Homepage

Indiana University Bloomington Libraries

Distributed Education Services

Getting Started

IUB Network ID/Password and Library Barcode

- Having a Network ID/Password and Library Barcode will allow you to fully utilize the services the library has to offer. The Network ID and password allow you to search most of the IUB databases. The Library Barcode allows you to check out materials from the IU Bloomington Libraries and have them delivered to you at a distance. To request the Library Barcode, please fill out this Request Form.

  If you have questions about whether you have existing IUB computing accounts, please visit Network ID Services to see a summary of your accounts.

Search our library catalog (IUCAT) and journal indexes

Book and Article Delivery

- **Information and Request Forms**
- **Renew Materials**
  - **Via a web form.**
  - **Through e-mail at libcirc@indiana.edu.**
  - **By Phone at 812-855-4673.**

Learning How to Conduct Good Research

- **Online Tutorials**

Printable Database Instructions

- **Basic Search Techniques**
- **IUCAT**
- **Various Databases**

Citing Sources

  How to Cite Electronic Sources
- **APA**
  - **Print Sources**

- o Electronic Resources
- MLA
  - o Print Sources
  - o Electronic Resources

Writing Help

- How to Write a Thesis Statement
- How to Avoid Plagiarism
- How to Evaluate Information

Research Assistance

- Call 1-888-258-6977 for personal, one-on-one assistance.

URL:http://www.indiana.edu/~libdist/start.html
Last updated: 24 May 2004
Comments: libdist@indiana.edu
Copyright 1997, The Trustees of Indiana University

The University of
KANSAS

Printer Friendly

Libraries A-Z A B C D E F G H I J K L M N O P Q R S T U V W X
Y Z

LIBRARIES

Information Gateway

Library Catalog

Course Reserves

Databases A-Z

E-journals

Request Materials

Libraries Home

KU Home

 HawkHelp
phone - email - chat

Search libraries web
Search popular databases
Find a book
[   ] Go

Library Home >> Distance
Learning

Distance Learning Information Services supports instruction, study, and research by members of the KU community who are involved in distance learning activities, including Web-based courses, faculty members on sabbatical leave, and students participating in the Study Abroad program. Contact Nancy Burich nburich@ku.edu, Coordinator, with your questions, suggestions and comments.

Student Resources	**Faculty Resources**	**Research Tutorials**
How do I find information? • KU Resources • Resources beyond KU **Services available** • Reserve • Circulation (check out materials) **Getting books, articles, etc.** • Document Delivery (getting books & articles from a KU library) • Interlibrary Loan (getting books & articles from a non-KU library) •Tips for Getting Materials Interlibrary Loan & Document Delivery **Study Abroad** • Library Services **How do I get help?** • Reference • Research 101 • Technical Issues	**Getting Information to Students** • Library Instruction options • Reserve **Copyright & plagiarism resources** • Avoiding Plagiarism • KU Copyright and Plagiarism • Copyrighted material within Blackboard • Distance Learning Issues • Resources for Faculty • Libraries databases for Journal Articles **New Resources** • KU Libraries at your fingertips! Take a peek for fast research help • Current Research@ University of Kansas Digital library of dissertations and theses **Sabatical Leave** • Library Services **More about distance learning** • KU Distance Learning Courses • Distance Learning Web Links (not at KU) **Distance Learning Help**	**Tutorials for Online Research** Blackboard Tutorial ✓ Tips ERIC Tutorial ✓ Tips Expanded Academic Tutorial ✓ Tips Finding E-journals Tutorial Finding a Database ✓ Tips Libraries Homepage Philosopher's Index ✓ Tips Social Work Abstracts ✓ Tips Voyager Web of Science ✓ Tips **Handouts** •Fair Use and Blackboard •Sample Database Searches

Welcome to DLLS

New distance learner or distance professor?

If you are enrolled in or teaching a University of Louisville distance education program/course for the Summer 2005 semester, please click on the "Get Started" button (above left) to request a username and password for library access from U of L's Office of Distance Learning Library Services (DLLS).

Password not working?

The library username and password is valid only for a specified length of time. The library password is different than any password that may be required for your course.

Library passwords issued for Spring 2005 courses in U of L distance education programs were deactivated on Monday, May 9, 2005. Passwords for students and professors in continuing U of L international and Ph.D. programs were immediately reactivated. If your password no longer works and you are a returning distance learner, please click on the "Get Started" button (above left) to request a new DLLS password.

Greetings!

U of L distance education programs currently eligible for Distance Learning Library Services are listed under the "Get Started" button on the DLLS toolbar above.

The following library services are available for University of Louisville distance learners after authentication of enrollment in a U of L distance education program:

- off-campus access to guided reading required or suggested by course professors (electronic course reserve)
- off-campus access (from non-U of L internet addresses) to electronic databases of library resources for self-directed research
- delivery of library resources not available immediately online, including:
    - retrieval and copying of items from U of L library collections (or from elsewhere, if necessary)
    - mailing, faxing or emailing of requested items to distance learners and professors
    - Costs: Items that cost under $25.00 per item are delivered at no cost to the individual . Any costs above $25.00 per item are billed to the individual following pre-approval.

To begin your journey into Distance Learning Library Services, simply click on the Get Started button located on the toolbar at the top of this page.

We look forward to serving your library research needs.

Sharon M. Edge, Professor
Office of Distance Learning Library Services
University of Louisville

UNIVERSITY OF MANITOBA

http://www.umanitoba.ca/libraries/distance_education/

 university of manitoba **Elizabeth Dafoe Library**

Library Catalogue   Library   UMInfo [   ] [SEARCH]

THE UNIVERSITY   DIRECTORIES   MAPS   FACULTIES   MY UMINFO

 THE UNIVERSITY OF MANITOBA LIBRARIES

Library catalogue ▸
Reserves / E-Reserves
My library account ▸
Databases / E-Journals ▸
E-Theses
Google Scholar
University Archives ▸
Facilities ▸
UM Libraries ▸
Services at your library
Ask us

 Chat Help

About Dafoe ▸
Dafoe Update
New Books
Reserves/E-Reserves
Document Delivery ▸
Audio Video Catalogue
FAQ

Information for Faculty

 Ask us

 UMinfo

UMinfo

People

Google

[   ]
[SEARCH]

Off-Campus & Distance Education Library Services

Bringing the Library to YOU

What's New?

For Students

For Faculty

 Request ONLINE

What's New
For Students
For Faculty

Off-Campus & Distance
Education Library Service

Elizabeth Dafoe Library
University of Manitoba
Winnipeg, MB
R3T 2N2

Phone: (204) 474-9183

In Manitoba: 1-800-432-1960
ext. 9183

In Canada: 1-888-216-7011
ext.9183

Fax: (204) 474-7570

E-mail:
dafoe_disted@umanitoba.ca

Elizabeth Dafoe Library
The University of Manitoba Libraries
Winnipeg, MB, Canada R3T 2N2
Phone: (204) 474-9544, Fax: (204) 474-7577
Questions or Comments? Email Webmaster
© 1997, University of Manitoba Libraries

Michigan State University Libraries

Guide for Online and Off-Campus Nursing Students

Arlene M. Weismantel, MILS
Health Sciences Librarian
Michigan State University Libraries
weisman1@mail.lib.msu.edu

August 2004

http://www.lib.msu.edu/staff/weisman1/OnlineNursingGuide.pdf

MICHIGAN STATE UNIVERSITY

www.lib.msu.edu/staff/weisman1/OnlineNursingGuide.pdf

TABLE OF CONTENTS

Introduction

The *Michigan State University Libraries' Guide for Online and Off-Campus Nursing Students* has two essential purposes. The first goal of this *Guide* is to help you successfully complete your class assignments; the second goal is to provide you with some of the skills necessary to become a lifelong learner who is able to provide the highest quality patient care throughout your career.

New knowledge in nursing and medicine is gained every day through the research process. The information you learn in your classes may be cutting-edge today, but will soon be obsolete. Therefore, one of the most important skills you can learn during your nursing education is how to locate, evaluate and use the most current nursing knowledge.

This *Guide* is intended to help you be independent and self-sufficient; that is, to teach you how to find the information you need yourself. However, a *Guide* such as this is not comprehensive and information technology changes so rapidly that some of the information presented here will be come outdated during the year. If you feel that you are spending as much time learning the process of finding information as absorbing the content, you may be right. Do not hesitate to call Library Distance Learning Services at 1-800-500-1554 if you have questions.

NCSU LIBRARIES

| Home | Services | Research Resources | About the Libraries | NC State |
| Search Catalog | Database Finder | E-journal Finder | | |

DLS Home Page

SERVICES
Catalogs
Book & Article Delivery
E-resources
E-books
Faculty Services
Full List of Services

COURSE RESOURCES
Course Reserves
Course Pages

HELP
Ask a Librarian
Are You a Distance Learner?
Frequently Asked Questions
Visiting NCSU Libraries

LINKS
Distance Learning Courses
Engineering Online
Distance Learning Links
Other Libraries
Contacts

DISTANCE LEARNING SERVICES

Welcome to Distance Learning Services! All library services at NC State University are available to the distance education community, and we make every effort to meet the needs of distance learners at NC State University. Some of our key services and features of use to distance learners include:

- Order books and articles - regardless of location.

- Thousands of electronic journals and databases are available from off campus.

- Ask a Librarian - use email, telephone (**toll-free: 1-877-601-0590**), online chat, fax, or mail to ask reference questions.

Features

- The WebCT Libraries Link helps faculty add customized Libraries resources to any WebCT course.

- Learn how to find articles.

- Use the E-journal Finder to locate electronic versions of journals, magazines, and newspapers.

Contacts

Staff Contact Information

Phone and Fax:
1-877-601-0590 toll-free
(919) 513-3655 telephone
(919) 515-8264 fax (attn: DLS)

Mailing Address:
Distance Learning Services
NCSU Libraries
2205 Hillsborough Street
Box 7111
Raleigh, NC 27695-7111

Distance Education at NCSU, Main number: (919) 515-9030, Toll free: (866) 467-8283

Search Catalog | Database Finder | E-journal Finder | Ask a Librarian | Search Website | Site Index
Home | Services | Research Resources | About the Libraries | NC State

Copyright | Disclaimer

Last Modified: 2005-04-04
Questions/Comments to LibWebTeam
URL: http://www.lib.ncsu.edu/distance/

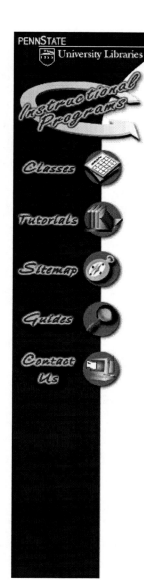

PENNSTATE
University Libraries

Students *Faculty* *Visitors* *Librarians*

Welcome to University Libraries' site for World Campus and Distance Education!

This gateway site provides information about how to access and make the most of the many University Libraries' services and resources available to you.

This site requires Flash 6.0 for viewing. If you do not have Flash 6.0, you may download it here.

Click here to access the Libraries Resources and Services for World Campus/Distance Education site with animation.

If you would like to view this site as text only, without animation, click here. (You may switch between the animated version of this site and the text-only version at any time.)

If you have any questions or comments regarding this tutorial, please contact Sylvia DeSantis in University Libraries' Instructional Programs at smd13@psu.edu or 814-865-5093.

Penn State Home | University Libraries | LIAS | Instructional Programs
Classes | Tutorials | Sitemap | Guides | Contact Us
Students | Faculty | Visitors | Librarians

Please address questions and comments to Instructional Programs.
This page was last updated February, 2004.

©The Pennsylvania State University, 2000

LibCat | Chiron | E-Resources | Site Map | Questions? | Search Library Site >> [   ] GO!

Texas A&M University Libraries
College Station, Texas 77843-5000 (979) 845-5741

| Home | Services | Research Support | Collections | About the Libraries | Giving to the Libraries | Help | My Portal |

Services » Additional Services » Distance Education

- Binding Services
- Clinical Outreach
- **Distance Education**
- EdNET
- GIS (Geographical Information Systems)
- Lockers
- Patent Services
- Lost & Found
- Records Management
- Writing Center
- Thesis Office

Distance Education Services

The Texas A&M University Libraries are responsible for providing library services, which mirror services provided on-campus, to their distance education students. It is the libraries' mission to provide access to as many resources and services as possible to support curriculum-related teaching, research, and other scholarly endeavors to their distance education students. Texas A&M University Libraries, --YOUR LIBRARIES --, invite and encourage you to use the many resources and services the libraries offer. The staff is ready to help you.

Eligibility for Services

Distance Library Services are available to off-campus TAMU students who are enrolled in TAMU distance education degree program or credit course.

Off-Campus courses are defined as those courses delivered outside the TAMU College Station campus. Students must be attending classes via:

- Distance Education degree or credit program delivered by TAMU colleges and departments
- Independent study (off-campus)
- Internet-delivered classes, TTVN, and off-campus face-to-face classes

Distance Library Services are not available to:

- Students attending classes on the TAMU College Station campus
- Persons not affiliated with TAMU

Important Services

- Online Catalogs (LibCat, Chiron)

  -The TAMU libraries online catalogs enable you to locate books, journals, and other library materials owned by the libraries.

- E-Resource Locator

  -The E-Resource Locator allows you to search databases/ Indexes and access directly e-journals and e-books. NetID (aka NEO account) is required to use this service.

- Document Delivery Services (deliverEdocs)

  -DeliverEdocs is an online document supply system that allows you to request items of your need. Articles will be delivered to you electronically and books will be sent to your home.

- Reference and Research Services

  -You may submit your reference questions using Ask a Reference Question service or AskNow Virtual Reference. The library subject specialists are available for in-depth reference questions. You are also encouraged to contact reference librarians at 1-888-843-0044 or 1-800-968-2638 for your information needs.

- Electronic Reserves

  -The service provides access to materials placed on Electronic Reserves by your instructors. NetID or NEO account is required for this service.

- Class Guides

    -The Class Guides provides course-specific library resources and research strategies in the specified classes.

- Texshare Card Program

  -The program allows you to check out library materials at your local academic or public library in Texas. Online application for a Texshare card is available. Your Texshare card must be renewed each semester.

- Net Library

  - A web-based library of over 11,000 full-text popular, professional and scholarly books that you can browse or read online. You will be prompted for your NetID/NEO account in order to user this service.

Contact Information

Library Distance Learning Services
Phone: 979-845-6281
E-mail: ZLiu@lib-gw.tamu.edu
Fax: 979-862-4759
Office Hours: Monday - Friday 8:00am - 5:00PM

State of Texas | Compact with Texans | Statewide Search | Public Information Act
Texas A&M University | Privacy Statement | Accessibility Rules | Contact Webmaster

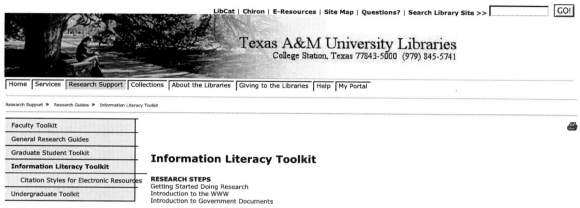

LibCat | Chiron | E-Resources | Site Map | Questions? | Search Library Site >> [   ] [GO!]

Texas A&M University Libraries
College Station, Texas 77843-5000 (979) 845-5741

| Home | Services | Research Support | Collections | About the Libraries | Giving to the Libraries | Help | My Portal |

Research Support » Research Guides » Information Literacy Toolkit

Faculty Toolkit

General Research Guides

Graduate Student Toolkit

Information Literacy Toolkit

    Citation Styles for Electronic Resources

Undergraduate Toolkit

Information Literacy Toolkit

RESEARCH STEPS
Getting Started Doing Research
Introduction to the WWW
Introduction to Government Documents

EVALUATING SOURCES
Evaluating Web Sources
Critically Analyzing Information Sources | Accompanying Checklist
Scholarly Journals vs. Popular Magazines

CITING SOURCES
Using the APA (American Psychological Association) Format
Using the CMOS (Chicago Manual of Style) Format
Using the MLA (Modern Language Association) Format
Using the Turabian Format
Using Endnotes in Turabian Documentation
Citation Guide for Electronic Resources
Citation Styles for WWW Sites
Intellectual Property, Fair Use, and Academic Integrity in an Electronic Environment

Copyright 2005 Texas A&M University Libraries.

State of Texas | Compact with Texans | Statewide Search | Public Information Act
Texas A&M University | Privacy Statement | Accessibility Rules | Contact Webmaster

WASHINGTON STATE UNIVERSITY

http://www.wsulibs.wsu.edu/electric/library/index2.html

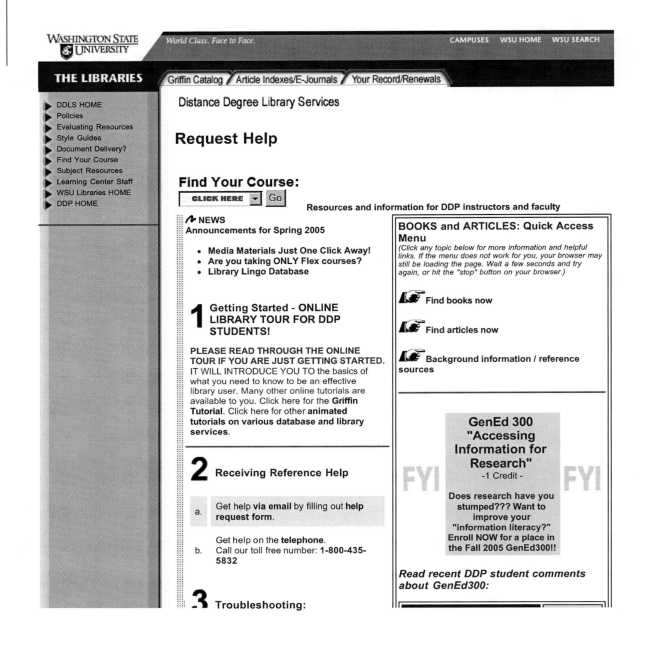

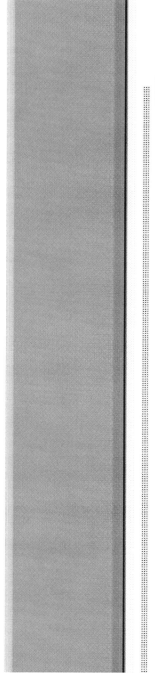

a. **Report technical problems.**

b. **I can't find the full text of the article I want.**

c. **ILLiad form to request articles unavailable online.**

d. **Erase your PIN (if you've forgotten it).**

To avoid PLAGIARISM check out these online **tutorials**.

"...(GenEd 300) should be a requirement.... (H)aving this class earlier would have not only saved me many hours wasted on frivolous searching, but would have increased my chance at a better grade!"

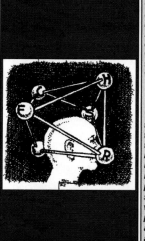

"...I feel very confident in my researching skills now, especially with all the tools we were given."

"... I know that this is the first time I have really understood how to perform a search, where to perform it and how to analyze what data was returned."

...read more comments about GenEd 300.

WSU FLEX STUDENTS

Are you a DDP Flex student who is not in the WSU Libraries' system? Click here to request access

These tours were built for use with Netscape version 4.73 or Higher or Internet Explorer version 5.0 or Higher. If you do not have either one of these web browsers, you may not be able to use all of the fuctions built into theses tours. If you need to upgrade your web browers click here for Netscape 7.02 or for Internet Explorer 6.0.

WSU Libraries Online Tour

Undergraduate DDP students

Welcome to the WSU Libraries Online Tour especially designed for WSU's undergraduate DDP students.

This tour will guide you to some of the central information you will need to effectively use the WSU Libraries. Among the topics covered in the tour are:

- How to access library materials from off-campus
- How to do a basic Griffin search
- How to access other databases for your research

The TOUR consists of three consecutive sections. You will first be introduced to the BASICS about the WSU Libraries. Section two, TRY ME, will challenge you to interactively navigate through many library resources. In the last section, REVIEW, you will test your library skills.

If you have questions or issues that aren't covered in the tour, please feel free to contact us.

ACRL Information Literacy Stardards

Contact us: Library Instruction (libinstr@wsu.edu) | (509) 335-7735 | Accessibility | Copyright | Policies
Distance Degree Library Services, P. O. Box 645610, WSU Libraries,
Washington State University, Pullman, Washington, 99164-5610 USA

Last updated on Thursday May 19th, 2005.
http://www.wsulibs.wsu.edu/electric/trainingmods/DDP_Student_Online_Tour/blankpage.html

Faculty Support Services

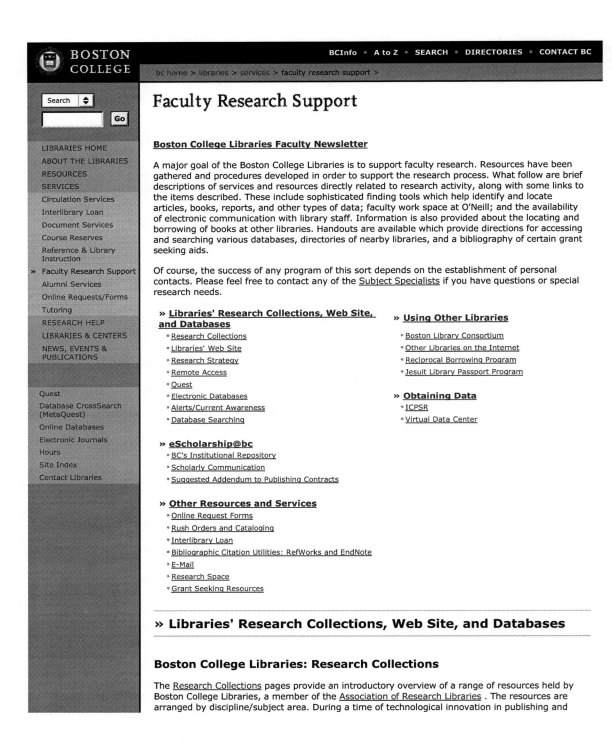

BOSTON COLLEGE

BCInfo ○ A to Z ○ SEARCH ○ DIRECTORIES ○ CONTACT BC

bc home > libraries > services > faculty research support >

Faculty Research Support

Search ▢
[Go]

LIBRARIES HOME
ABOUT THE LIBRARIES
RESOURCES
SERVICES
Circulation Services
Interlibrary Loan
Document Services
Course Reserves
Reference & Library
Instruction
» Faculty Research Support
Alumni Services
Online Requests/Forms
Tutoring
RESEARCH HELP
LIBRARIES & CENTERS
NEWS, EVENTS &
PUBLICATIONS

Quest
Database CrossSearch
(MetaQuest)
Online Databases
Electronic Journals
Hours
Site Index
Contact Libraries

Boston College Libraries Faculty Newsletter

A major goal of the Boston College Libraries is to support faculty research. Resources have been gathered and procedures developed in order to support the research process. What follow are brief descriptions of services and resources directly related to research activity, along with some links to the items described. These include sophisticated finding tools which help identify and locate articles, books, reports, and other types of data; faculty work space at O'Neill; and the availability of electronic communication with library staff. Information is also provided about the locating and borrowing of books at other libraries. Handouts are available which provide directions for accessing and searching various databases, directories of nearby libraries, and a bibliography of certain grant seeking aids.

Of course, the success of any program of this sort depends on the establishment of personal contacts. Please feel free to contact any of the Subject Specialists if you have questions or special research needs.

» Libraries' Research Collections, Web Site, and Databases
  ○ Research Collections
  ○ Libraries' Web Site
  ○ Research Strategy
  ○ Remote Access
  ○ Quest
  ○ Electronic Databases
  ○ Alerts/Current Awareness
  ○ Database Searching

» eScholarship@bc
  ○ BC's Institutional Repository
  ○ Scholarly Communication
  ○ Suggested Addendum to Publishing Contracts

» Other Resources and Services
  ○ Online Request Forms
  ○ Rush Orders and Cataloging
  ○ Interlibrary Loan
  ○ Bibliographic Citation Utilities: RefWorks and EndNote
  ○ E-Mail
  ○ Research Space
  ○ Grant Seeking Resources

» Using Other Libraries
  ○ Boston Library Consortium
  ○ Other Libraries on the Internet
  ○ Reciprocal Borrowing Program
  ○ Jesuit Library Passport Program

» Obtaining Data
  ○ ICPSR
  ○ Virtual Data Center

» Libraries' Research Collections, Web Site, and Databases

Boston College Libraries: Research Collections

The Research Collections pages provide an introductory overview of a range of resources held by Boston College Libraries, a member of the Association of Research Libraries . The resources are arranged by discipline/subject area. During a time of technological innovation in publishing and information delivery, the Boston College Libraries are developing a digital library of electronic resources essential to current academic scholarship and teaching. At the same time, the Libraries continue to add to the collections of books, journals, microforms, videos, and other kinds of materials which form the historic foundation of library holdings. Further information is available from the subject specialists who have helped build the collections and from the subject research guides available on the library web site.

[Top of Page]

The B.C. Libraries' World Wide Web Site

A growing number of research resources and services are available on the internet. Subject Specialists are continuing to identify internet sites and point to them via the Libraries' WWW pages. Web browsers such as Internet Explorer or Netscape Navigator can be used to locate a vast range of web sites, and to make direct access to off-campus computer databases such as library catalogs. The URL for the B.C. Libraries' site is: http://www.bc.edu/libraries/.

Also, check the links for **Resources**; these include links to

- Quest: Library Catalog
- MetaQuest
- Online Databases
- Electronic Journals
- Electronic Books
- Research Collections
- Research Guides
- Ready Reference
- Other Libraries

Elsewhere one may access Boston College Libraries' Digital Library Initiatives page which highlights new or existing digital services and research projects of particular importance to students and researchers.

[Top of Page]

A Note on Research Strategy

Researchers should know how recent the information offered by any database is and plan accordingly.   The following resources provide "early detection":

- WorldCat and RLIN (Fill in BC username & pin #) offer a great deal of current data regarding domestic publication; they contain bibliographic records for books published in the U.S. which are still in the publication process and have not yet reached libraries and bookstores.

- A number of databases (e.g. Quest , ingenta , ERIC , PsycINFO , and others) and collections of electronic journals (e.g. Cambridge University Press Journals , Oxford University Press Journals , and others) permit you to save a search profile/strategy. These are automated current awareness services that result, depending on the type of profile or strategy, in book citations, in table of contents of your chosen journals or a list of individual article citations being e-mailed directly to your e-mail box. (More information on automated alerts.)

N.B.: Updating frequency varies from database to database; it can be monthly, quarterly, or even annually.

When designing research strategy for an ongoing project, the researcher may want to consider how to keep up with information as well as to determine which resources provide the most recent information. Some resources allow the saving of search statements; saved terms or phrases can be run each time a database is updated. Call the appropriate Subject Specialist to find out about updating frequency and search saving features for any particular database.

[Top of Page]

Remote Access

Most databases available through the Boston College Libraries are restricted to the Boston College community. In order to access these databases from off-campus, you need to log in as a verified B.C. community member. For further information, please consult: Remote Access Information.

[Top of Page]

Quest

The web-based Quest is Boston College Libraries' state-of-the-art integrated library information system. Currently **Quest**'s main database is the Boston College's Library Catalog. Another **Quest** database is FACP - BC Faculty Publications Catalog a citation database of scholarly publications produced by Boston College faculty. Updated annually, **FACP** represents approximately 12,000 scholarly publications produced by full-time faculty members. Important features of the **Quest** system include:

- ability to renew or view items on loan
- to review recall and hold requests
- to customize the way results are displayed
- to set up an alert profile, a service that automatically sends out an e-mail list of new library acquisitions according to your area(s) of interest.

Quest can be accessed by terminals and microcomputers on and off campus. The URL for **Quest** is http://www.bc.edu/quest . For more information please contact any Subject Specialist or O'Neill's Reference Desk (x24472).

The results of most searches in **Quest** are organized by publication date, with the most recently published titles appearing first. This may help you find the latest material in your research areas. The Advanced Search technique allows you to search by year of publication, by language of the text, by format (e.g. journals & newspapers, electronic journals, microform, musical scores, archives/manuscripts, musical recordings, kit, realia, graphic, sound recordings, maps), by specific library location at Boston College, by publisher name and place, and by a number of other possible qualifiers. Please consult the relevant help screens in **Quest** for further information.

[Top of Page]

Electronic Databases

Numerous databases are available in the various B.C. Libraries, and increasingly on the Internet. Contact your Subject Specialist for the most recent information.   Also, consult the Online Databases page on the B.C. Libraries web site for an alphabetical list and a Subject Index for the databases arranged by discipline/category. Check the New Databases page periodically for the latest acquisitions.

SFX is a feature of a growing number of Boston College Libraries' databases. SFX allows you to go from a citation in a database and view a list of services available for that citation. Boston College uses the name and icon find it⊙ for this technology. The current services offered on the Find It Menu include:

- Link to full text from a database or electronic journal collection.
- Check Holdings in Quest, BC's Library Catalog.
- Search for the Author in a database.
- Send Questions and Comments about Find It to a BC Librarian.
- Get the Find It Frequently Asked Questions.

Not all of these services will appear when you click the Find It link. It depends on the database that you are using.;
You will only see find it⊙ (Find It) links after you have searched a particular database.

MetaQuest : A New Way For You To Manage & Search Across Databases
Now available on the Libraries' web site is MetaQuest , a new product that will help you manage your favorite resources and allow you to search across multiple databases at one time. MetaQuest provides access to all of the Libraries' web-based databases currently found on the Libraries' Online Databases page. In addition, MetaQuest allows you to customize a list of databases, so that each time you sign-in, your list will appear within a *My Resources* List. You can browse databases by subject and search up to eight databases at one time.

Whether you are researching psychology, art history, business, or nursing, MetaQuest will help you identify the appropriate resources for your research. You can search databases within MetaQuest by Author, Title, Subject, Year or All Fields. If you choose six databases to search, then all six will be searched at the same time and the results will be displayed for each database. You can select records and save them to your *e-Shelf* for up to 30 days, or you can e-mail or save records to a disk. MetaQuest also allows you to permanently save your search history, so each time you sign-in you can run previous searches that have been saved. For databases that are not searchable within MetaQuest you can connect to the database directly.

[Top of Page]

E-Mail Alerts/Current Awareness

Set up automated alerts.

A number of databases (e.g. Quest, ingenta, ERIC, PsycINFO , and others) and collections of electronic journals (e.g. Cambridge University Press Journals, Oxford University Press Journals, and others) permit you to save a search profile/strategy. These are automated current awareness services that result, depending on the type of profile or strategy, in book citations, in table of contents of your chosen journals or a list of individual article citations being e-mailed directly to your e-mail box.

Particular mention may be made of Quest. **Quest** is Boston College Libraries' Catalog for all books, journals, CD-ROM, audio-visual materials and other cataloged items. It provides a **QuestAlert** feature that allows users to define a search profile. Based on this profile, **Quest** automatically sends out an e-mail list of new publications that may be of interest to the user.

Another important database providing an alerts feature is ingenta . This database provides table of contents information (over 13 million article citations) taken from over 27,000 current journals and magazines in a very diverse range of disciplines. Journals are indexed within 24 hours of receipt. Coverage is from late 1988 to the present and includes journals in the arts, humanities, social sciences, and the sciences. The journals indexed encompass a broad range from popular to the more scholarly.

Some Useful Alerting Features in ingenta:

Research Alerts
Research alerts are a subject and author alerting service where you can create up to 25

keyword or author search alerts. You enter the keywords or author names you want to search against and, on a weekly basis, **ingenta** runs your searches against any new content in the system and sends you the new citations by email.

Table of Content Alerts
Sometimes known as TOC alerts, table of content alerts allow you to receive by e-mail table of contents of new issues of your chosen publications as they are available on **ingenta**. One may select up to 50 titles per year.

Find further information about Quest, ingenta, and other databases and collections of journals providing alert features by consulting the guide for automated alerts .

[Top of Page]

Online Database Searching

A number of online information resources which provide citations and abstracts of published literature, statistical tables, full-text of selected articles, directories, and business/financial data are searchable by professional library staff. Searches are performed after initial interviews with a librarian have determined the specific subject needs of the researcher. Contact your Subject Specialist for more information.

[Top of Page]

» eScholarship@bc

BC's Institutional Repository

eScholarship@BC is a digital repository of scholarly material produced by Boston College scholars and researchers. The repository is a central online system that manages the storage, access, and preservation of a variety of materials, including working papers, preprints, postprints, and theses and dissertations. eScholarship@BC is currently a pilot project administered by the Boston College Libraries. During the 2004-2005 academic year, the libraries will be working with a small number of academic departments and research centers to demonstrate the capabilities of the repository, develop policies and procedures for participation in the repository, and develop a plan for a campus-wide rollout of eScholarship@BC.

A key component of the eScholarship at Boston College initiative is the Libraries' commitment to and support for open access to scholarly literature. The Libraries are a signatory of the Budapest Open Access Initiative, which defines open access as the "free availability on the public internet" of scholarly literature "without financial, legal, or technical barriers other than those inseparable from gaining access to the internet itself." Open access benefits scholars by maximizing the visibility, influence, and benefit of their research. More details about eScholarship@BC is available at Background Information and Resources.

[Top of Page]

Boston College Libraries and Scholarly Communication

BC Libraries are swiftly and enthusiastically expanding their digital and print resources. The dynamic library and information environment is extremely exciting and favorable to the promotion of teaching, research, and scholarship. There are also difficulties in solving some of the challenges posed by the greatly growing amount and cost of resources. For an overview of some of these challenges, please see the web page Scholarly Communication . This page provides links to selected sites containing articles, papers, programs, association home pages etc. pertaining to many aspects of scholarly communication. Please don't hesitate to get in touch with Brendan

Rapple: rappleb@bc.edu or with any other of the library subject specialists if you have any questions regarding the role of research in the evolving scholarly communication climate.

[Top of Page]

Suggested Addendum to Publishing Contracts

Before signing a publishing contract, Boston College faculty, students and staff should consider carefully how the contract might later affect their usage of the published work in their teaching and research. It is important that Boston College authors retain the right to include the published work in a coursepack, to place it on their personal web pages and to post and update it in a scholarly e-print server. Frequently, however, the terms of a publisher's contract have access restrictions on work being used in such ways. Consequently, we recommend that all authors take care to assign the rights to their work in a manner that permits them to use the work freely, and permits their Boston College colleagues to use the work freely, in their teaching and research at Boston College. Accordingly, we encourage authors to request that the following "scholarship dissemination-friendly" addendum be added to their contracts:

> "I retain the right to use this work, in whole or in part, in my personal teaching and research activities, for my colleagues at Boston College to use this work, in whole or in part, in their personal teaching and research activities. I also retain the right to post the work, in whole or in part, on my personal non-commercial web site as well as the right to post the work, in whole or in part, in free public e-print servers hosted by Boston College or by scholarly societies and associations."

For more information on this and related scholarly communication issues please see Boston College Libraries' Scholarly Communications page. This page also links to a Copyright and Intellectual Property page.

[Top of Page]

» Other Resources and Services

Online Request Forms

The Libraries' web site offers several electronic forms which can assist researchers in acquiring materials. The following forms can be accessed by choosing the **Online Requests/Forms** option in the **Quick Links** pulldown menu on the Libraries' home page):

- **View/Renew Loans**: A list of books, etc. currently charged out to you.
- **Recall/Delivery Requests**: A list of recall and delivery requests that you have placed.
- **Interlibrary Loan Book Request**: Complete this form to request materials via Interlibrary Loan.
- **Interlibrary Loan Journal Article Request**: Complete this form to request an article via Interlibrary Loan.
- **Locate and Photocopy Request**: Complete this form to request a photocopy of an article or book chapter. This service is available when classes are in session. The cost is 20 cents per page. (Only available for items in O'Neill Library).
- **Request Item from Law Library**: Complete this form to request delivery of a book or a photocopy from the following remote libraries: NEDL, K-C, NRC or the Law Library.
- **Ask a Reference Question**: Complete this form to ask our reference librarians a question.
- **Request a Research Consultation**: Complete this form to request a research consultation with a subject specialist.
- **Library Instruction Request Form:** Complete this form to request a formal library instruction session.
- **Request Data from ICPSR**: Complete this form to request data from the Inter-university

Consortium for Political and Social Research (ICPSR).

- **Recommend Library Materials**: Use this form if you would like to recommend that the library purchase specific materials.

To have a book rush ordered or to have a book that is designated as "in process" in **Quest** rush catalogued, go to Rush Ordering/Cataloging below.

[Top of Page]

Rush Ordering/Cataloging

Any book not yet received and cataloged by Boston College Libraries may be ordered through the appropriate Subject Specialist , or by using the electronic form **Recommend Library Materials** (accessible by choosing the **Online Requests/Forms** option in the **Quick Links** pulldown menu on the Libraries' home page). Quest may inform you that a certain title is "on order." When one accesses the Holdings information for the title, one may click "request" to ask that the title be rush ordered and that you be notified when the item arrives. If using the **Recommend Library Materials** form, use the "Additional Comments" box to request a rush order.

If **Quest** informs you that the book is "in process," click on the "request" link on the holdings screen and follow instructions. This initiates a message that requests that the book be rush catalogued. On the other hand, one may fill out one of the RUSH slips available at the Circulation Desk. The book should be available within 3-5 business days.

[Top of Page]

Interlibrary Loan

One may request the Interlibrary Loan Office (3rd floor O'Neill) to obtain material not possessed by the O'Neill Library. Details of the book, article, etc. may be filled out in person at the ILL Office or by using an electronic Interlibrary Loan Form accessible on the InterLibrary Loan page . One may also initiate an ILL request from several OCLC First Search databases, WorldCat, a database of over 50 million items, being perhaps the most prominent. The Law Library processes borrowing requests for the Boston College law school faculty, staff and students.

[Top of Page]

Bibliographic Citation Utilities

RefWorks

RefWorks is a web-based bibliographic citation management tool that assists users in creating personal collections of citations by easily importing references from online databases . These references can then be inserted into papers and RefWorks will automatically format the footnotes and bibliography in many different styles including MLA, APA, Turabian and Chicago. As a web-based product, RefWorks is available to users across various platforms including Windows, Mac, Unix, etc. and accessible from any workstation with an Internet connection. Read more about RefWorks.

Endnote

EndNote is a bibliographic mangement software program that assists users in collecting, organizing and presenting citations to articles, books, Web sites and more. Many databases can be searched remotely through EndNote using connection files , or a native database may be searched and the citation information saved to your desktop. These records can then be imported into your EndNote library using filters . Product information and support can be found on the EndNote web site.

[Top of Page]

E-Mail

A quick and convenient method of on-campus communication is electronic mail or e-mail. It can be used to reach the Subject Specialists . You may consider using this mode for placing rush orders or sending messages concerning your research needs. For information on how to obtain an e-mail account, a faculty member can contact the Technology Consultant assigned to their department or area.

Note: The University provides information about getting an e-mail account and setting up the necessary software -- access the IT Help Center and choose "Email".

[Top of Page]

Research Space

Space for faculty research is available on the 5th level of O'Neill Library. Offices are available as well as carrels in an open space area. Contact the office of Michael Smyer , Dean & Associate Vice President for Research to arrange use of a carrel or office. There are two carrels in the open space area available on a first come, first served basis. Go to the O'Neill Administrative Office, Room 410 in O'Neill Library for access information.

[Top of Page]

Grant Seeking Resources

There are numerous web sites which provide information about available research grant support . The types of information include grant application deadlines, the names of contact persons and their phone numbers and addresses, the subject scope of the foundation's or agency's interests, and details about projects recently funded by any particular foundation or agency. The Office of Sponsored Programs (OSP) (x23344) also searches an online database not available at O'Neill Library called SPIN . In addition, the Office of Sponsored Programs has a link to the Grant Writer's Toolbox , a collection of valuable links to help Grant Writers develop successful applications. Any thorough effort to identify the possible sources of research funding might make use of all these online services. Please contact any Subject Specialist to have a search done on relevant databases available at O'Neill.

NOTE: O'Neill Library has numerous print publications which may assist you in locating potential funding sources.

[Top of Page]

» Using Other Libraries

Boston Library Consortium - Member Library Catalogs & Borrowing Privileges

The Boston Library Consortium (BLC) Gateway provides access to the individual online catalogs of all the BLC members (Boston Public Library Research Collections, Boston University, Brandeis University, Brown University, Marine Biological Laboratory/Woods Hole Oceanographic Institution, MIT, Massachusetts State Library, Northeastern, Tufts University, UMass/Amherst, UMass/Boston,

UMass/Dartmouth, UMass/Lowell, UMass/Medical, University of New Hampshire, Wellesley College, Williams College, University of Connecticut, and Boston College). This gateway may be useful after a WorldCat or a RLIN (Fill in BC username & pin #) search. WorldCat and RLIN can tell you what libraries may have a particular title. Then, by searching the online library catalog of the library which owns the item, you can check to see if it is available for borrowing.

Faculty members requiring research materials not available at Boston College may receive Boston Library Consortium (BLC) cards which will enable them to borrow material from any of the BLC member libraries. The forms are at O'Neill's Reference Desk. Check with the Theology department about borrowing from any of the BTI member libraries. A directory of the BTI libraries is available.

[Top of Page]

Other Libraries on the Internet

More than 50 library catalogs showing books and other materials of more than 400 Massachusetts libraries can be searched from the Massachusetts Library Information Network (MLIN) . Library materials held by most Massachusetts public libraries and by approximately 30 academic libraries are to be found in the online catalogs of the nine large automated resource sharing networks.

More and more of the world's great libraries are making their catalogs available on the Internet. The Library of Congress has a new web interface for its catalog. The British Library Public Catalogue (BLPC) contains details of over 10 million books and other material covering every aspect of human thought from 1450 onwards. The Canadian Libraries Gateway provides a centralized window to Canadian libraries of all types and sizes. For national libraries in Europe, there is Gabriel, a gateway with links for their online catalogs. There is also a web page of links to national libraries throughout the world provided by IFLA, the International Federation of Library Associations and Institutions. Web access to other libraries around the world is available through LibWeb. National Library Catalogues Worldwide is a useful page for accessing scores of national libraries throughout the world.

HOLLIS, the online union catalog of Harvard University Libraries, is a database containing records for more than 14 million of the diverse items in the collections of the Harvard libraries. (Harvard is not a member of the Boston Library Consortium). Library Catalogs in the U.S. is an A to Z list of telnet connections to academic libraries

N.B.: Whenever using one of these catalogs, make sure to check what they include. Only a portion of their collections or the more recent acquisitions may have bibliographic records available by this method of access.

[Top of Page]

Reciprocal Faculty Borrowing Program

The Reciprocal Faculty Borrowing Program (RFBP) is a program that allows faculty members of participating institutions borrowing privileges and on-site access to the collections of some of the most important research libraries in North America. To promote and facilitate scholarly research and communication among members of their faculties, the university research libraries that are members of the Association of Research Libraries and participate in OCLC (a nonprofit membership organization serving 41,000 libraries in 82 countries and territories around the world) banded together to provide this enhanced access.

Materials may be used on the premises of the owning library or may be borrowed, depending on the policies of the lending library. Privileges vary from library to library and the lending library determines whether a user under this program will have on-site use and/or borrowing. With this privilege also come responsibilities. Boston College faculty visiting other institutions must observe the regulations of the lending library; return materials, in person or by mail, within the loan period established by the lending library; and pay all fines or other charges incurred due to late return or damage to materials

If you are visiting another part of the country for research purposes and think that you might want to use an academic library in that area, stop by the O'Neill Library reference services desk for a list of participating institutions and more information. You must have an RFBP borrowing card, issued by Boston College, to gain access or borrow from a participating institution. For more information contact any Subject Specialist. The number of participating libraries is amost two hundred.

[Top of Page]

Jesuit Library Passport Program

The libraries of the Jesuit institutions represented in the Association of Jesuit Colleges and Universities (AJCU) have joined together to provide a nationwide reciprocal borrowing program for the faculty of each institution. Faculty members have on-site access to the collective holdings of 28 Jesuit institutions. In addition, if a Boston College faculty member visits one of these institutions, the library will grant the visitor borrowing privileges. Before visiting, the faculty member must complete an AJCU Direct Reciprocal Library Borrower Form, available in the O'Neill Library at the main Circulation Desk. Then take the completed, signed form with you to the participating library, together with your Boston College photo ID. Please remember that borrowing privileges are determined by the host lending library and may or may not be similar to your borrowing privileges at Boston College.

[Top of Page]

» Obtaining Data

ICPSR

Faculty, students and members of the B.C. community can now directly download data sets from the Inter-University Consortium for Political and Social Research (ICPSR) web site. ICPSR is an archive of thousands of data sets on topics covering education, health care, demographics, social indicators, political behavior, and much more. Find data by searching the database by keyword, investigating agency or by an ICPSR study number. The web site also highlights special data collections for major research areas such as Education, Aging, Substance Abuse and Mental Health Data among others. Most data collections now have online codebooks, which are also searchable and downloadable. When an online version of documentation is not available, the library will acquire a print copy and add it to our collection. Faculty and students who have used ICPSR data for years will find it faster and easier to download the data themselves. To manage large data sets requiring additional space and research support, you may contact either Barbara Mento, mento@bc.edu or Rani Dalgin, dalgin@bc.edu, for further assistance.

Access instructions and links to the ICPSR catalog.

[Top of Page]

Virtual Data Center

The Virtual Data Center was developed to help faculty and students find and easily access data for both research and classroom work. The web site provides information about our data collection, support services for statistical analysis and descriptions and access information about statistical packages and data translation software.

Support services are provided by library professionals and Academic Technology Support consultants. Support services include assistance in locating data, customized class presentations on finding data, technical support for data sub-setting for research or customized class assignments, data translation, statistical software access and Geographic Information Systems software and instruction. Faculty are also invited to recommend data for acquisition with the Boston College

Statistical Dataset Suggestion Form.

A unique feature of the Center is a new Statistical Data Catalog which includes key research datasets available at Boston College. Records include descriptions of the data, available formats, documentation and direct download links whenever possible. Coverage includes U.S. and International data. While the catalog is expanding to support all disciplines, current datasets primarily support the areas of economics, finance, health care, education and social and economic indicators.

[Top of Page]

Last Revised: November 16, 2004

[Learn Our Web : Feedback : Top of Page]

Updated: April 21, 2005
Maintained: University Libraries
URL: http://www.bc.edu/libraries/services/faculty/
© 2005 The Trustees of Boston College. Legal

home > services > services for faculty

Services for Faculty

Listed below are some of the more popular services available at UGA Libraries with faculty in mind:

- Ask A Question
  Send your questions to UGA Libraries Email Reference Service.

-
  Borrowing Privileges
  Detailed explanation of faculty borrowing privileges including using an emissary to charge out books, privileges for faculty spouses and children, recalls, and much more.

-
  Collections/Departments
  An alphabetical directory of the Collections and Departments at UGA Libraries. Many have their own homepages which will list additional services offered.

-
  Disability Services
  Services and contact information for patrons with special needs.

-
  Distance Learning
  UGA Libraries resources and services of special interest to faculty members conducting distance learning classes.

-
  Faculty Liaison
  Learn to use electronic resources for your research. Also find out about software such as Endnote to organize the references you find.

-
  Instruction
  Find out about UGA Libraries' orientations, workshops, one-on-one conferences, and online research aids.

-
  Interlibrary Loan
  How to request materials from other libraries.

-

Services

A - Z
Students
Faculty
Alumni
General Public

UNIVERSITY OF GEORGIA

http://www.libs.uga.edu/services/facultyservices.html

Newsletter
Libraries' Links is a listserv newsletter dedicated to helping you find out about online research databases available through the UGA Libraries.

- Password for GALILEO
Instructions for accessing the current GALILEO password and your library account information.

- Photographic Services
Provides quality photographic and imaging services to University faculty, staff, library patrons and students. Also, offers digital imaging, 35mm and medium-format copy work, and black and white photography.

- Reserve Procedures
Instruction for placing materials on Reserve.

- Reserves Catalog
Search for reserved library materials by instructor, department or course.

- Wireless Network
Using a wireless-equipped laptop, you can login to the wireless network with your UGA MyID at both the Main and Science Libraries.

 Last Updated:1/10/2005

The University of Georgia Libraries   home   sitemap   search

home > ask a question

Ask A Question

Email	• Email short factual questions to us through our webform. We also provide guidance about finding and choosing appropriate information sources through email. Please be as specific as possible about your information needs.
Telephone	• Main Library Reference - (706) 542-3251 • Science Reference - (706) 542-0698 • Student Learning Center - (706) 542-4673 • Distance Learning - (877) 314-5560 (toll free) • Access Services (Circulation) - (706) 542-3256 For other units consult our alphabetical list of departments.
Chat	• Chat online with a UGA Reference Librarian. This service is Available Monday-Thursday from 8 AM until 9 PM and Friday from 8 AM until 5 PM.
In Person	• Stop by one of our reference desks. Hours and directions.
Research Conferences	• Research Conferences are available for UGA faculty, staff, and students needing help with major projects or in-depth research. Distance students should consult the Help For Distance Learners page.
FAQs	• Check our FAQs for commonly asked questions.

Privacy Policy

 Last Updated:6/2/2005

home > faculty liaison

Faculty Liaison

The Faculty Liaison for Electronic Library Services is available to the university community, especially UGA faculty, staff and graduate students to share current information about licensed electronic resources and how to exploit them in research, instruction and service.

Individual meetings by appointment in campus offices focus on the desktop databases and full-text options most relevant to one's research and teaching.

Training in the integration of bibliography manager software such as Endnote, ProCite and Reference Manager with electronic resources is provided in one-to-one or group seminars. Customization and ease of use with research databases licensed by the UGA Libraries and GALILEO is a primary goal.

Additional services include but are not limited to:

- Strategies for locating citations to one's (or someone else's) publications
- Efficiencies in desktop management of research database access, e-mail streamlining
- Identification of publishing opportunities
- Referrals to specific librarians/library services

Faculty Liaison

Endnote
Citation Search
Research Tips
Contact Information

Last Updated:3/17/2005

The University of Georgia Libraries   home   sitemap   search

home > faculty liaison > citation search

Faculty Liaison

Endnote

Citation Search
  -databases and

Library Resources and Your Publications

Do you want to know

...who has cited an article which is important to your research ?

...who has cited your own publications?

...the acceptance rate of a journal?

...the circulation of a journal?

...the Impact Factor of the top journals in a discipline as determined by ISI's formula?

This information and more is available in library resources, many web-based and searchable from your office computer.

The following categories of online and print resources will identify related research for a literature review, as well as assist in your decisions about manuscript submissions and provide information for your dossier.

strategies
  -web of science tips
  -journal profiles
  -help with citation

1. Citation Indexing -- numerous sources to determine who is citing whose research or related research papers

2. Profiles of Scholarly Journals -- sources for circulation statistics, manuscript acceptance rates, timetable from submission to publication, peer review specifics, etc.

3. Impact Factors -- one of several significant analytical elements in Journal Citation Reports. The preceding link is for use on-campus only; from off-campus, visit GALILEO , type current password. After screen rebuild, search Journal Citation Reports in A-Z list or type in Find a Database by Name box.

searches
Research Tips
Contact Information

 Last Updated:8/20/2004

UNIVERSITY OF GEORGIA

http://www.libs.uga.edu/ref/instruction/confer.html

The University of Georgia Libraries   home   sitemap   search

home > reference > classes and conferences > research conferences

Research Conferences

An individualized orientation to the UGA Libraries is available by appointment. Students beginning a master's thesis, a doctoral dissertation, or a major research paper, and faculty/staff are encouraged to use this service.

Use the e-mail request form or ask for a "Library Research Conference" request form at either the Main or Science Libraries Reference Desk.

Referrals to special collections of the Libraries, such as the Hargrett Library or the Map Room, will be made when appropriate.

Reference

Department

Research Central
Ask A Question
Classes and

Conferences
  -class instruction
  -library class

   resources
   -research conferences
   -tours & orientations
   -for-credit classes
Disability Services
Distance Learning
Hours
How to Reach Us
Staff

 Last Updated:7/1/2004

home > reference > distance learning > distance learning links

Distance Learning Links

Research Stations and Affiliated Campuses

- Coastal Plain Experiment Station (Tifton.)

- Griffin Campus Library (College of Agricultural and Environmental Sciences.)

- Skidaway Institute of Oceanography.

- Gwinnett University Center Library.

Technology Resources

- Enterprise Information Technology Services (EITS) - EITS provides computing and networking support for UGA students and faculty.

- Element K - Information on online computer training modules available through UGA (My ID required).

- EndNote - Bibliographic management software freely available to UGA faculty, staff and students. A UGA UGA Library Account is required.

Other Resources

- UGA Book Store.

- University of Georgia Distance Learning Links - Links to distance learning programs available through UGA and the University System of Georgia.

- Advanced Learning Technologies (ALT) - This division of the Board of Regents of the University System of Georgia supports instructional technology activities of system faculty and staff through a variety of projects and activities.

- Southern Regional Educational Board Electronic Campus - This web site provides information on distance learning courses and degrees offered by over 200 Southern colleges and universities, including UGA.

(877) 314-5560 Toll Free | Email | Fax (706) 583-0268

Reference

Department

Research Central
Ask A Question
Classes and

Conferences
Disability Services
Distance Learning
Hours
How to Reach Us
Staff

UNIVERSITY OF IOWA

http://www.lib.uiowa.edu/disted/consultation.html

| ⊠ |
| Request Consultation |

DISTANCE-EDUCATION RESEARCH CONSULTATION SERVICE

The University of Iowa Libraries offers a consultation service to students and faculty involved in distance education. The purpose of this service is to provide professional advice on research methodlogies and strategies so that students and faculty obtain information pertinent to their research projects.

The librarian will assist in identifying information needs, constructing effective search techniques, locating information, and using print, microform, CD-ROM, online, and Internet sites. Resources include subject bibliographies, library catalogs, periodical and subject indexes, dissertation lists, electronic texts, and reference sources pertinent to the research project.

CONSULTATION APPOINTMENTS

Individual consultation appointments with Stephen Dew, the Coordinator of Library Services for Distance Education, may be made by a toll-free telephone call (**877-807-9587**), by e-mail (stephen-dew@uiowa.edu), or by using the form provided below. Please be as specific as possible about your research topic. Also, it is helpful to be very specific about your preferred contact method (e-mail or telephone).

The appointment date and time will be arranged.

CONSULTATION APPOINTMENT FORM

Complete all sections and press the "SUBMIT" button at the end of the form. The information you provide will be electronically submitted to the Coordinator of Library Services for Distance Education.

RESEARCHER'S NAME:

DEPARTMENT OR CLASS:

TELEPHONE:

EMAIL ADDRESS:

PROJECT LEVEL (check one):

    Undergraduate   Master's Level   Doctoral Level   Other

ASSIGNMENT DUE DATE & PROJECT DESCRIPTION
(please describe your research project in detail):

RESEARCH STATUS (check one):

I'm just starting my research.
I've done the preliminaries, but need to find more information
Other:

Please list sources already consulted:

Submit Form   Clear Form

Return to Distance-Education Library Services Home Page

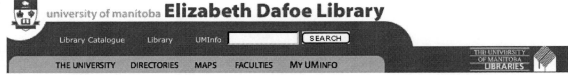

university of manitoba **Elizabeth Dafoe Library**

| Library Catalogue | Library | UMInfo | [   ] [SEARCH] |

THE UNIVERSITY   DIRECTORIES   MAPS   FACULTIES   MY UMINFO

THE UNIVERSITY
OF MANITOBA
LIBRARIES

Library catalogue »
Reserves / E-Reserves
My library account »
Databases / E-Journals »
E-Theses
Google Scholar
University Archives »
Facilities »
UM Libraries »
Services at your library
Ask us

Chat Help

About Dafoe »
Dafoe Update
New Books
Reserves/E-Reserves
Document Delivery »
Audio Video Catalogue
FAQ

Information for Faculty

For Faculty

- Curriculum and Resource Development
- Instruction
- E-Reserves
- Document Delivery

Request
ONLINE

Curriculum and Resource Development

The Off-Campus Librarian is eager to assist faculty and instructional developers in providing current and quality materials for their course content and supplemental readings. You may contact the librarian at the OCDE Library Services office.

The University of Manitoba Libraries also has subject specialists in each discipline who manage the collection and offer instruction classes.

A list of librarian subject specialists is available at: umanitoba.ca/ libraries/units/collections/bibliographers_list/sub2.php

Instruction

Library staff conduct tours and provide in-depth group instruction in the library, in classrooms and in computer labs. Topics covered include learning how to use BISON (the Libraries' online catalogue), NETDOC (networked databases), print periodical indexes, and how to search the Internet, etc.

Teaching staff may also request classroom sessions on subject-specific resources.
For more information, contact a librarian at one of the libraries.

A list of UM Libraries is available at: umanitoba.ca/libraries/units

E-Reserves

E-Reserves provides remote access to reserve course materials in electronic format which previously were only available in print from the Libraries.

Faculty members may submit their own materials directly on the ERes system using an assigned account, or they can choose to have the library staff at Elizabeth Dafoe Library process the materials.

For more information...

Document Delivery

Interlibrary loan is a transaction in which library material, or a copy of the library material, is made available by one library to another upon request.
Once you have confirmed through BISON that UM Libraries does not own the item, you may request the item directly using Document Delivery's online form.

What's New
For Students
For Faculty

Off-Campus & Distance
Education Library Service

Elizabeth Dafoe Library
University of Manitoba
Winnipeg, MB
R3T 2N2

Phone: (204) 474-9183

In MB: 1-800-432-1960 ext. 9183

In Canada: 1-888-216-7011 ext.9183

Fax: (204) 474-7570

E-mail:
dafoe_disted@umanitoba.ca

ⓂⓊLibraries

Distance Learning Support Service
Home   Electronic Resources   Faculty Services   Index

- Who may request materials?

- How to find information on a topic

- How to access electronic resources

- How to obtain materials

- Circulation Information
    - What books do I have checked out?
    - What do the MU Libraries charge for overdue, recalled, and lost books?

- Ask a question
- More information

- Other universities that offer Distance Learning

- Health Sciences Students & Faculty: see the HSL Distance Education Site

Distance Learning students often have a wide variety of questions about the MU Libraries Distance Learning Support Service. If you have a question that isn't covered here, please contact the Ellis Reference Desk 573-882-4581 or send email to: *ellisref@missouri.edu* .

- **Who may request materials?**

    - University of Missouri-Columbia distance education students may request material to be sent out to them by the Libraries. This service is not available to residents of central Missouri (Audrain, Boone, Callaway, Cole, Cooper, Howard, Moniteau, and Randolph counties).
    - All students enrolled in MU's Distance Learning Programs are eligible for Reciprocal Borrowing privileges through MERLIN (other UM campuses and St. Louis University) and MOBIUS (academic libraries in the state of Missouri).
    - Students not residing in the United States may be eligible for borrowing privileges at local libraries, depending upon those libraries' policies.

- **What do the MU Libraries charge for overdue, recalled, and lost books?**
    - After any item on loan is recalled, you will not be able to borrow anything else from the Libraries until you return the item, and you will be liable for a $2 per day fine (up to $100). Further delay will result in an invoice for the cost of replacement for a further $175
    - If you have any query about notices or have lost a book, notify the lending library immediately by contacting your Liaison Librarian.
    - Please note: The Libraries will pay for sending books out; students pay for returning them.
    - Other campuses may charge for overdue items which have not been recalled.

MU Libraries

Library Services for Faculty Instruction and Research

Frequently Asked Questions

- Check out Materials
- Contacts
- Copy Service
- Hours and Locations
- Printing in Library Computing Sites
- Request Books, Journals and Articles not available locally
- Show me how to....

- Campus Libraries, Collections and Archives
- Campus Library Committee
- Distance Learning
- Donate Books and Journals
- Related Services at MU
- Scholarly Communication Issues

Focus on Research

- Subject Librarian Assistance
- Library Catalogs
- Electronic Databases
- Electronic Journals
- Grants
- Publishers (Books and Journals)
- Remote Access

Workshops, Tours and Instruction

- Copyright
- Course Reserves
  - ERes (Electronic Reserves)
- Library Instruction
- Tutorials for E- Resources

Frequently Asked Questions

Circulation Services

- Check out materials
- Renew materials
- View my circulation record
- Request a proxy card for my student assistant

Request Additional Books, Journals and Articles

- Request-a-book service through MERLIN or MOBIUS

- Request MU-owned journals stored off-site (Annex/UMLD)
- Request books from the Annex/UMLD

- Borrow books/articles from other libraries (Interlibrary Loan)
  - Electronic ILL request forms

- Recommend a book or journal for purchase -- contact your subject or branch librarian.

- Locate a new book being processed -- contact your subject or branch librarian.

- On Campus Document Retrieval Service: Fee-based service for journal articles available on campus.

Subject Librarian Assistance

- Reference Services
  - Reference services are provided by Ellis Library and all branch libraries.
  - Subject Librarians by subject   By Librarian

- Ellis Library Reference
  - Ask a Reference Question by E-mail
    The Ellis Library Reference Staff will answer your question, if it can be answered, the next working day. Please be sure to include your name and e-mail address. Do not assume it will be added automatically by the computer. Submit a question.

  - Ask a Reference Question by Phone
    Call (573) 882-4581

8:00 AM - 12:00 AM	Monday - Wednesday
8:00 AM - 10:00 PM	Thursday
8:00 AM - 5:00 PM	Friday
10:00 AM - 5:00 PM	Saturday
1:00 PM - 12:00 AM	Sunday

  - Ask a Reference Question by chatting live with a Reference Librarian
    - http://mulibraries.missouri.edu/refservices/contactus.htm

1:00 PM - 9:00 PM	Monday - Thursday
1:00 PM - 5:00 PM	Friday

    top

Workshops, Tours and Instruction

Copyright | Course Reserves | Guides and Tutorials | Schedule a Class or Tour

Course Reserves / Electronic Reserves

- **Electronic Reserve -- ERes (FAX number: 884-5073)**
  - Request for an ERes account
    - Guidelines for ERes

  - Link directly to e-journals and to full-text articles -- creating online bibliographies
    - Academic Journal Policy Database
      (database of links to publishers' journal policies)

- **Print Reserve Services (see individual branch libraries for branch policies)**
  - Ellis Library Reserve Desk

  - Print materials - Course Reserve Request Form (Ellis Library)

- o Print materials - Course Reserve Request Form (Engineering Library)
- o Print materials - Course Reserve Request Form (Math Library)

- **Copy Service**
- **Custom Publishing: course packets** (University Bookstores)

Schedule a Class or Tour

- Learning@MULibraries
  - o Learning@MULibraries Request Form
- Subject Guides to Library Collections
  - o Guide to resources and the research process for the web

- Ellis Library Tours
- Ellis Library Instruction Page
- Individual Consultations
  - o Subject Librarians by Subject
  - o Subject Librarians by Name
- HSL Workshops, Journalism Instruction (See branch libraries web pages)

Assignment Calculator (University of Minnesota)

top

How-to Guides and Tutorials for Electronic Resources

- MU Libraries Research Tutorial
- Guide to Internet Resources and the Research Process
- MERLIN/MOBIUS Tutorial
- net.TUTOR   (OSU Libraries guide to searching the web)
- Tutorial for Learning how to use Ovid databases (UMSL)

Copyright

top

Focus on Research

Data Archives | Electronic Resources | Grants | Library Catalogs | Publishers,
Journal Title Databases | Reference Management Software | Search Assistance | Translations

Collections

- **Library Catalogs**
    - MERLIN Catalog (University of Missouri/St. Louis University libraries)
        - (tutorial)
    - MOBIUS (Missouri academic libraries)
    - Additional national catalogs and databases

- **Electronic Resources** (See also specific branch library web pages, e.g., HSL)

    - Access electronic resources from off campus
    - Databases by Name
    - Databases by Subject
    - Electronic Journals

- **Health Sciences Library**
    - HSL Databases
    - HSL E-Books
    - HSL E-Journals

- **Search Assistance --**
    - Subject Guides to Library Collections
    - Subject Librarians by Subject
    - Subject Librarians by Librarian

Publishers, Journal Title Lists and Databases

- MU Electronic Journals
- MERLIN journal title search
- **Ulrich's Periodical Directory** MU Only

- AcqWeb's Directory of Publishers and Vendors
- **WorldCat (national book/journal title catalog)** MU Only
- JAS (Journal Abbreviation Sources)

Grants

- MU Funding Agency Information
- Community of Science Funding Opportunities
- CRISP (Computer Retrieval of Information on Scientific Projects)
- Science and technology grants and funding
- GrantSource Library: Proposal Writing Help
- Proposal Writing Help

top

Related Services at MU

- Academic Support Center
- ET@MO (Educational Technologies)
- Academic Retention Services
- Campus Writing Program

- IATS
- Program for Excellence in Teaching
- University Extension

- Intensive English Program
- The Learning Center
- Online Writery
- Student Success Center

Donate books and journals

MU Libraries -- Gifts

- Contact your subject or branch librarian.
- Call Gifts for information. (882-4834)
- Your old books (information about rare books)

Heartland Book Bank

The Heartland Book Bank is a non-profit organization, run mostly by retired librarians. They channel donated books to prisons, abuse shelters, etc. The Book Bank has no way to pick up the books so the donor must provide transportation or shipping to get the books there.

Jo Ann Harper
Heartland Book Bank
1425 Oak (AT&T building) Room 160
Kansas City, MO
816-472-5600

Overseas

- Donation Programs for Books, Journals and Media (SUNY-Buffalo)
- Book Donation Programs (Sabre Foundation)
- The East & Central Europe Journal Donation Project
- Book donations to the Third World (A list, compiled by a student at Lafayette, posted as a message to the Journal of Service-Learning Discussion Group)
- Brother's Brother Foundation
- Bridge to Asia (A place you can donate books to Asia and mail them library rate or UPS)

Foreign Trade Services
Pier 23
San Francisco CA   94111

MU Libraries
University of Missouri–Columbia

Page revised: 02/25/05 * webmaster
Copyright ©2000 Curators MU * EEO/ADA

top

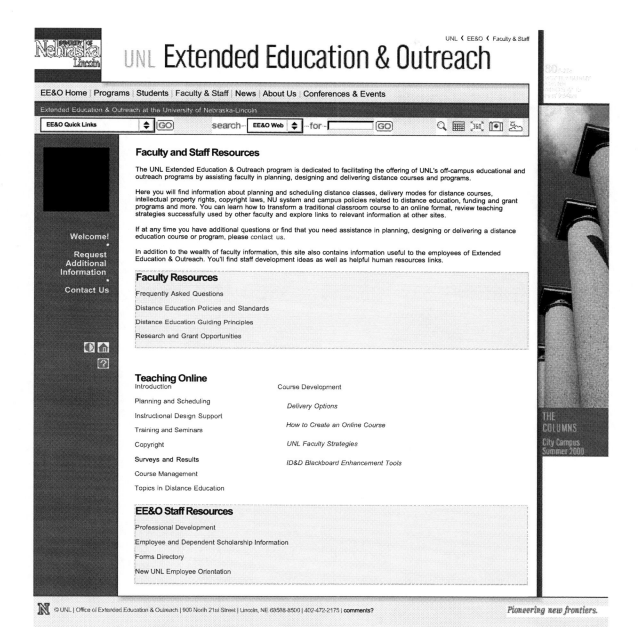

UNL ‹ EE&O ‹ Faculty & Staff

UNL Extended Education & Outreach

EE&O Home | Programs | Students | Faculty & Staff | News | About Us | Conferences & Events

Extended Education & Outreach at the University of Nebraska-Lincoln

EE&O Quick Links ▼ GO   search EE&O Web ▼ for GO

Welcome!

Request Additional Information

Contact Us

Faculty and Staff Resources

The UNL Extended Education & Outreach program is dedicated to facilitating the offering of UNL's off-campus educational and outreach programs by assisting faculty in planning, designing and delivering distance courses and programs.

Here you will find information about planning and scheduling distance classes, delivery modes for distance courses, intellectual property rights, copyright laws, NU system and campus policies related to distance education, funding and grant programs and more. You can learn how to transform a traditional classroom course to an online format, review teaching strategies successfully used by other faculty and explore links to relevant information at other sites.

If at any time you have additional questions or find that you need assistance in planning, designing or delivering a distance education course or program, please contact us.

In addition to the wealth of faculty information, this site also contains information useful to the employees of Extended Education & Outreach. You'll find staff development ideas as well as helpful human resources links.

Faculty Resources

Frequently Asked Questions

Distance Education Policies and Standards

Distance Education Guiding Principles

Research and Grant Opportunities

Teaching Online

Introduction   Course Development

Planning and Scheduling

Instructional Design Support   *Delivery Options*

Training and Seminars   *How to Create an Online Course*

Copyright   *UNL Faculty Strategies*

Surveys and Results

Course Management   *ID&D Blackboard Enhancement Tools*

Topics in Distance Education

EE&O Staff Resources

Professional Development

Employee and Dependent Scholarship Information

Forms Directory

New UNL Employee Orientation

THE COLUMNS

City Campus Summer 2000

Ⓝ © UNL | Office of Extended Education & Outreach | 900 North 21st Street | Lincoln, NE 68588-8500 | 402-472-2175 | comments?

Pioneering new frontiers.

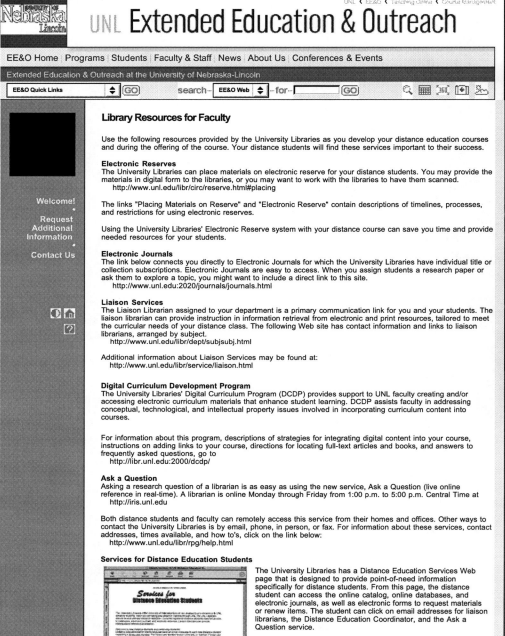

UNL ‹ EE&O ‹ Teaching Online ‹ Course Management

UNL Extended Education & Outreach

EE&O Home | Programs | Students | Faculty & Staff | News | About Us | Conferences & Events

Extended Education & Outreach at the University of Nebraska-Lincoln

EE&O Quick Links ▢ GO   search — EE&O Web ▢ —for— [   ] GO

Welcome!
·
Request
Additional
Information
·
Contact Us

JOHNNY
CARSON
Comedian
Class of 1949

Library Resources for Faculty

Use the following resources provided by the University Libraries as you develop your distance education courses and during the offering of the course. Your distance students will find these services important to their success.

Electronic Reserves
The University Libraries can place materials on electronic reserve for your distance students. You may provide the materials in digital form to the libraries, or you may want to work with the libraries to have them scanned.
http://www.unl.edu/libr/circ/reserve.html#placing

The links "Placing Materials on Reserve" and "Electronic Reserve" contain descriptions of timelines, processes, and restrictions for using electronic reserves.

Using the University Libraries' Electronic Reserve system with your distance course can save you time and provide needed resources for your students.

Electronic Journals
The link below connects you directly to Electronic Journals for which the University Libraries have individual title or collection subscriptions. Electronic Journals are easy to access. When you assign students a research paper or ask them to explore a topic, you might want to include a direct link to this site.
http://www.unl.edu:2020/journals/journals.html

Liaison Services
The Liaison Librarian assigned to your department is a primary communication link for you and your students. The liaison librarian can provide instruction in information retrieval from electronic and print resources, tailored to meet the curricular needs of your distance class. The following Web site has contact information and links to liaison librarians, arranged by subject.
http://www.unl.edu/libr/dept/subjsubj.html

Additional information about Liaison Services may be found at:
http://www.unl.edu/libr/service/liaison.html

Digital Curriculum Development Program
The University Libraries' Digital Curriculum Program (DCDP) provides support to UNL faculty creating and/or accessing electronic curriculum materials that enhance student learning. DCDP assists faculty in addressing conceptual, technological, and intellectual property issues involved in incorporating curriculum content into courses.

For information about this program, descriptions of strategies for integrating digital content into your course, instructions on adding links to your course, directions for locating full-text articles and books, and answers to frequently asked questions, go to
http://libr.unl.edu:2000/dcdp/

Ask a Question
Asking a research question of a librarian is as easy as using the new service, Ask a Question (live online reference in real-time). A librarian is online Monday through Friday from 1:00 p.m. to 5:00 p.m. Central Time at
http://iris.unl.edu

Both distance students and faculty can remotely access this service from their homes and offices. Other ways to contact the University Libraries is by email, phone, in person, or fax. For information about these services, contact addresses, times available, and how to's, click on the link below:
http://www.unl.edu/libr/rpg/help.html

Services for Distance Education Students

The University Libraries has a Distance Education Services Web page that is designed to provide point-of-need information specifically for distance students. From this page, the distance student can access the online catalog, online databases, and electronic journals, as well as electronic forms to request materials or renew items. The student can click on email addresses for liaison librarians, the Distance Education Coordinator, and the Ask a Question service.

At the start of each semester, all currently enrolled distance education students are sent an email message that outlines the library resources and services. The Distance Education Web Site is

Click to view a larger image

http://www.unl.edu/libr/de/de_main.htm

noted in this message.

You are encouraged to include a link to the Distance Education Services Web page in your courses.

UNL Libraries Link on Blackboard

Click to view a larger image

All students also have access to the University Libraries through a direct link in Blackboard. You may find reminding students about this link through your announcements or in instructions for projects a good way to alert students to the benefits of using library resources.

Information Your Student Recieves About the Libraries
Please visit the Courses and Degree Programs Catalog [link to catalog] to find out more about the information your students receive on library services.

NU ID#s: As the university shifts from using the social security number as student ID number, distance students will be issued an NU ID# when they first register for a class. Distance students will be informed of that number, which they will need in order to access the library. Eventually they will use the NU ID# for registration. Students receive an application for an NCard which they may request. Lincoln students need to get an NCard for direct library access.

Contact Information
For more information about the University Libraries' Distance Education Services, please contact:

Kate Adams, Distance Education Coordinator
University Libraries
kadams1@unl.edu
(402) 472-2560

Home | Services | Research Resources | About the Libraries | NC State

DLS Home Page

SERVICES
Catalogs
Book & Article Delivery
E-resources
E-books
Faculty Services
Full List of Services

COURSE RESOURCES
Course Reserves
Course Pages

HELP
Ask a Librarian
Are You a Distance Learner?
Frequently Asked Questions
Visiting NCSU Libraries

LINKS
Distance Learning Courses
Engineering Online
Distance Learning Links
Other Libraries
Contacts

DISTANCE LEARNING SERVICES

Faculty Services

Don't leave the library out of your distance learning courses! The NCSU Libraries is committed to providing full services to students, no matter where they are or the means by which they take classes. We are also committed to helping faculty find ways for their students to use library resources effectively. If your students can't come to the libraries - the libraries will go to them. Services include:

Online Guides to Library and Information Resources

Reference librarians can create customized online guides to Library and Information Resources for your course. For example, see reference librarian Karen Grigg's library guide for a plant pathology course, or see reference librarian Cindy Levine's library guide for a philosophy course.

The WebCT Libraries Link describes how customized resources from the NCSU Libraries can be added to any WebCT course.

Library User Instruction

Librarians are available to offer library instruction sessions (teaching your students how to use library resources) via various delivery options, including visits to off-campus locations. For more information, please contact Kim Duckett by phone (919-513-3653) or by e-mail at kim_duckett@ncsu.edu.

If you have any additional instructional needs not listed in our description of library services for distance learning, please contact the Distance Learning Services Department. We will be glad to consult with you to find solutions.

Learning Technology Service (LTS)

LTS supports instructional tools such as WebCT and WolfWare; consults with faculty about putting courses online, instructional design, site design, and project planning; provides a digitization lab and a usability lab; and offers workshops.

NC State Distance Education Faculty Services

Search Catalog | Database Finder | E-journal Finder | Ask a Librarian | Search Website | Site Index
Home | Services | Research Resources | About the Libraries | NC State

Copyright | Disclaimer

Last Modified: 2005-04-04
Questions/Comments to LibWebTeam
URL: http://www.lib.ncsu.edu/distance/faculty.html

PENN STATE | ONLINE

GETTING STARTED | FINANCIAL AID | CONTACT US

CURRENT STUDENTS ▶ ENTER

| Home | Degrees | Certificates | Course Catalog | Student Services | About Us |

WORLD CAMPUS HOME » ABOUT US » RESOURCES FOR FACULTY

ABOUT PENN STATE WORLD CAMPUS

OUR MISSION

HISTORY

ORGANIZATION OVERVIEW

RESOURCES FOR FACULTY

   Faculty Development Philosophy

   Faculty Development 101

   Faculty Development Calendar

   Conferences and Related Organizations

   Reports and Resources

   Instructional Design Contact Information

FAST FACTS

PRESS ROOM

PARTNERSHIPS

EMPLOYMENT

PENN STATE OUTREACH

Resources for Faculty

Recognizing that a primary key to the success of an online teaching and learning program is a skilled and competent faculty, Penn State's World Campus has sponsored a faculty development initiative since 1995. The primary goal of the Faculty Development Program is to build a teaching and learning community of faculty and staff who can effectively author, design, develop, and deliver distance education courses via Penn State's World Campus.

A rich set of resources is available to assist Penn State faculty when teaching distance learners. These resources include:

- access to one-to-one faculty development
- faculty development online course
- hands-on technical training
- a variety of Internet resources, audio or face-to-face faculty development programs and conferences related to distance education

The Faculty Development Program serves as a bridge between the instructional design and development process and the faculty. The Instructional Design and Development (ID&D) unit of the World Campus works closely with the faculty to produce quality distance education courses that enhance the educational experience of the World Campus students to better meet their needs.

Search all of Penn State

GO

Home | Degrees | Certificates | Course Catalog | Student Services | About Us

Text Only Version | Privacy and Legal Statements | Copyright

Welcome to the Libraries' instructional web pages for **Faculty**

Quick Links

Tips for Creating Assignments

Virtual Research: Where the Web and Library Meet

Research Guides by Subject

Research Guides by Course

LEAP Summer Program

Services:

Did you know that you can have a librarian teach a session for your class? E-mail a request!

Browse through the English 15 Research Toolbox for assistance in orienting your English 15 students to the library and its resources.

Are you looking for media equipment or videos to enhance a class? Visit MediaTech!

Resources:

- ANGEL
- Library Locations
- Librarians by Subject (University Park)
- Commonwealth College and Campus Librarian

Need Help?

ASK!

Refer your first -year students to a site created just for them!

First-year Seminar Site!

(Requires at least Flash Player 5)

Penn State Home | University Libraries | LIAS | Instructional Programs
Classes | Tutorials | Sitemap | Guides | Contact Us
Students | Faculty | Visitors | Librarians

Please address questions and comments to Instructional Programs.
This page was last updated April, 2004.

© 2000 The Pennsylvania State University

LibCat | Chiron | E-Resources | Site Map | Questions? | Search Library Site >> [_____] GO!

Texas A&M University Libraries
College Station, Texas 77843-5000 (979) 845-5741

| Home | Services | Research Support | Collections | About the Libraries | Giving to the Libraries | Help | My Portal |

Research Support » Class Resources » FACULTY LEARNING COMMUNITY » Resources for Writing and Learning

Resources for Writing and Learning

| Workshop Resources |

| Center for Teaching Excellence | University Writing Center | TAMU Libraries |

WORKSHOP RESOURCES ^

* Syllabus and Agenda (Dialogue on Writing for Thinking and Learning -Summer 2004)
* Bibliography for Writing Across the Curriculum
* Bibliography for Critical Thinking   *Coming Soon!*

CENTER FOR TEACHING EXCELLENCE ^

* Link to the Center for Teaching Excellence

UNIVERSITY WRITING CENTER ^

* Link to the University Writing Center's Resources for Faculty

TAMU LIBRARIES ^

Starting Points

* TAMU Libraries Homepage
* Faculty Guide to the TAMU Libraries
* Undergraduate and Graduate Guides to the TAMU Libraries

Research Assistance and Class Instruction: Consultations, Library Orientations, and Instructional Sessions

* Reference assistance (online, by phone, in person)
* Request a consultation, class, or online class guide
* Directory of Subject Specialist Librarians

Research Guides

* Writing Subject Guide
* Citing Sources Tutorial and Handouts
* Information Literacy Toolkit (Steps in the research process, How to evaluate information, etc.)
* See a list of current Class Guides and Subject Guides or Request a Class Guide be made for your course

Course Reserves

* Put items on Reserve for your course

 **WASHINGTON STATE UNIVERSITY**

World Class. Face to Face.   CAMPUSES   WSU HOME   WSU SEARCH   myWSU

THE LIBRARIES / Griffin Catalog / Article Indexes/E-Journals / Your Record/Renewals

Libraries HOME
Search/Site Map
Hours/Phone
Contact Us
Ask a Question
Interlibrary Loans
Subject Resources
Reference Shelf
Classes & Handouts
Assistive Technology
About WSU Libraries
  Services
  Policies
  Departments
New Books
Libraries FAQ
News/Exhibits/Events
Other Library Catalogs
Giving to the Libraries

The Libraries - Your Information & Resources Gateway

WSU Library Instruction

Creating Effective Library Assignments

Keys to creating and executing a successful library based assignment:

General Principles and Guidelines:	Subject Area Specialist (Librarian) Contact:
• Identify a purpose or rationale for the assignment that is clearly communicated to the students • Make sure the assignment is closely tied to the course content to provide relevance • Check with the WSU Libraries' **Subject Area Resources** and **Subject Area Guides** to learn of relevant resources for your assignment • Work through the assignment yourself • Be sure that each resource listed on your assignment has the complete name of the item, accurate usage of terminology is a must • Create assignments so that a large number of students are not trying to get access to a very small number of resources	• Check with your **Subject Area Specialist** (librarian) to get an idea about available resources and potential resources limitations • Check with your **Subject Area Specialist** (librarian) about putting heavily used materials on reserve • Contact your **Subject Area Specialist** (librarian) to schedule a course-integrated instruction session • Contact your **Subject Area Specialist** (librarian) to see about putting a paper copy of your assignment at the reference desk • Encourage your students to stop by the Reference & Information Desk to get help if they need assistance

How the WSU Libraries help Instructors of DDP Courses

Consultation on assignment approach, links to databases, etc. to facilitate distance student research and access to information.
(contact Jane Scales, the Distance Learning Librarian, scales@wsu.edu...)

• Electronic reserves for your students (***more information...***)

• "Course page" with instructions and links to helpful databases for your students (***example...***)

• Bibliographic style links (***examples...***)

• Online Subject Resources (***more information...***)

• Virtual Reference Shelf (***resources...***)

How the WSU Libraries help DDP Students

• Online Tutorials to teach Information Literacy & Research Skills (***examples...***)

• Document Delivery of Books from Griffin and Summit, and Iliad items (***policies...***)

• Access to hundreds of online databases (***Article Indexes / E-journals page...***)

• Access to Electronic Books (ebooks) *(link to **NetLibrary** and **NetLibrary tutorial**...)*

• Reference assistance via phone or email (***policies...***)

Contact us: **Library Instruction (libinstr@wsu.edu)** | (509) 335-7735 |
Accessibility | Copyright | Policies
Distance Degree Library Services, P. O. Box 645610, **WSU Libraries,**
Washington State University, Pullman, Washington, 99164-5610 USA

Last updated on Thursday May 19th, 2005.
http://www.wsulibs.wsu.edu/electric/library/instructors.htm

Distance Learning Assessment

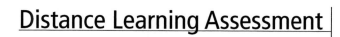

Distance Learning Faculty Survey
UGA Libraries – April 2004

Dear Distance Education Faculty Member:

Thank you for taking the time to complete this brief survey. Your input will help us better serve the Distance Learning community at UGA and is greatly appreciated.

1.) Beginning Fall 2004, your students can link from the University of Georgia Libraries catalog to a combined catalog for all the public college and university libraries in the state of Georgia. They may use the **Request** option in this combined catalog to request materials from any of these libraries, as well as the UGA Libraries through a delivery service. Do you think your students will make use of this service?
http://giluc.usg.edu/

       Yes   No

1A.) If you answered "No" to Question #1, which of the following options would you say is the most likely reason?

       A.) Lack of awareness of the service   B.) They don't need it

2.) Do you know that your students can link to a subject pathfinder for online resources in your discipline from the Libraries homepage?
http://www.libs.uga.edu/researchcentral/index.html

       Yes   No

3.) What School or College are you affiliated with? | College of Agricultural and Environmental Sciences ⬍ |

4.) Do you know that 300+ databases provided by the Libraries through the GALILEO platform are configured for remote, off-campus users, provided that the students are in the UGA Registrar's database?
http://www.galileo.usg.edu/

       Yes   No

5.) Do you know how to direct your students to the current GALILEO password for this remote service?

       Yes   No

6.) Have you ever looked at the Libraries Distance Learning web site?
http://www.libs.uga.edu/ref/dl/index.html

       Yes   No

7.) If you assign research projects in your distance education classes, do you provide your students the URL for the University Libraries web site on your course page?
http://www.libs.uga.edu/

       Yes   No   N/A

8.) What services would you like to see the Libraries provide your distance education students?

       Phone Consultation   On-line chat service   Interactive, web-based tutorials   Class Instruction sessions

9.) Please provide any comments or suggestions for improving services to distance education students and faculty in the box below.

Printer Friendly

Libraries A-Z A B C D E F G H I J K L M N O P Q R S T U V W X
Y Z

LIBRARIES

Information Gateway

Library Catalog

Course Reserves

Databases A-Z

E-journals

Request Materials

Libraries Home

KU Home

HawkHelp
phone - email - chat

Search libraries web

Search popular databases

Find a book

[   ] **Go**

KU Libraries Assessment Activities

The development of an assessment plan was one of the success factors identified in the KU Libraries Strategic Plan of 2000. In establishing an ongoing program of assessment activities, the Libraries hope to further our understanding of user needs and of the services, collections, and staff skills that will meet these needs.

- **Assessment Council Members**

- **Meeting Minutes**

- **Fall 2004 Freshman Survey Results**

- **Guidelines for providing assessment INCENTIVES (.doc)**

- **Powerpoint Presentation by Steve Hiller 3/8/04 (.ppt)**
  Steve Hiller meeting w/Assessment Council notes - AM (.doc)
  Steve Hiller meeting w/Assessment Council notes - PM (.doc)

- **LibQUAL+ Survey Information**

- **LibQUAL+ Survey Results (.pdf)**

  The results of our Spring 2003 LibQUAL+(TM) survey are available above in Adobe Acrobat PDF format. To view this file, you must have installed **version 5.0 or above** of the free Acrobat Reader, which can be downloaded from Adobe. If you experience problems viewing these files directly in your web browser, save them to your hard drive before opening them.

- **Assessment Task Force Report - submitted 2/18/03 (.doc)**

- **Deans response to Task Force Report 3/11/03**

The University of Kansas
Libraries
Lawrence, KS 66045
785.864.3506

Contact Us - © 2005 The University of Kansas : DMCA
This file was updated Friday March 25 2005

Position Descriptions

INDIANA UNIVERSITY LIBRARIES
Bloomington, Indiana 47405

LIBRARY FACULTY POSITION DESCRIPTION FORM

Name: Anne Haynes   Years covered: 2004

Position Title: Associate Librarian, Reference Department; and Distributed Education Library Services Coordinator

Campus: Bloomington

Library/Branch/Department: Main Library/Reference Department

Immediate Supervisor(s): Ann Bristow/Frank Quinn

Department Head: Ann Bristow/Frank Quinn

I.   Primary responsibilities

Please list here, in tabular form, those duties which you regularly or occasionally perform on which the majority of your time is spent. The duties should be directly connected with the title of your position and the function of your department. If these duties include any significant one-time projects, please specify.

-- Provide assistance to faculty, students, library and university staff, university administrative offices, staff of other libraries, and other researchers worldwide in solving their research and information needs: at the Reference Desk, over the telephone, by electronic mail and virtual "chat" reference, and by individual appointment, using the 40,000+- volume printed reference collection and over 400 online citation and/or full-text databases on a variety of platforms (SilverPlatter, Ebsco, JSTOR, OVID, Wilson, Proquest, ISI, Bowker, IAC, ABC-CLIO, among many others); and many digital resources with separate search protocols (e.g., British Library, OCLC WorldCat, RLIN, phone books, poetry databases, statistical databases, image databases, etc.)

-- Provide library instruction each semester including teaching orientation sessions for classes, individually designed instructional sessions and tours, orientation sessions for visiting faculty and dignitaries, and workshops such as the Faculty and Graduate Student Updates and UITS STEPS classes.

--Lead the department in coordinating the delivery of Distributed Education (DE) library services to students and faculty. DE includes services to IUB Continuing Studies, School of Education, HPER and other academic programs offering credit courses to graduate and undergraduate students and faculty away from campus.

-- Work with other departments and individuals in the Libraries to monitor trends as well as plan and deliver services to students and faculty in the IUB DE environment.

-- Facilitate the online registration of new DE students for library services and provide reference services to them

-- Work with individual DE instructors as needed to provide bibliographic instruction to DE classes in the absence of a librarian with that subject expertise.

-- Maintain the Libraries' DE Web site (http://www.indiana.edu/~libdist/), which is the only entry to the Libraries for distance students.

-- Participate in the review and evaluation of the Reference collection: this includes purchase suggestions for new print resources and transfer and withdrawal recommendations. Also includes the trial analysis and evaluation of dozens of electronic resources.

II. Secondary responsibilities

Please list here, in tabular form, those duties which you regularly or occasionally perform but which do not require the majority of your time. These duties should include regularly scheduled departmental or administrative meetings, but should not include committee appointments unless service is ex-officio.

-- Participate in weekly department meetings, and in regular meetings of the Research Collections and Services Department/Academic Information Services and public services departments

-- Share responsibility for reviewing Internet Quick Reference Web pages

-- Receive and verify citations for all patron purchase suggestions submitted to the department; route these requests to the appropriate collection managers.

There are approximately 250 such requests a year.

-- Participate in training of department's Reference Assistants

-- Assume other responsibilities as needed

III.   Qualifications
Please list here any special qualifications for the completion of your primary responsibilities. If previous library experience is essential, please indicate its length and nature. Other qualifications might include language skills, advanced degrees in non-library areas, non-library experience, etc. If such qualifications would be merely helpful rather than essential, please do indicate.

-- Master's degree in Library / Information Science from an accredited institution

-- Experience working in reference services in an academic library

-- Experience with computer applications and electronic database searching

-- Experience with the Internet and World Wide Web

-- Experience in working with the public and in teaching groups and individuals

-- Knowledge of one or more foreign languages extremely helpful

THE UNIVERSITY OF MANITOBA LIBRARIES

Position Incumbent:

Position Title: Off-Campus Librarian

Department: Reference Services Section, Elizabeth Dafoe Library

A. ROLES AND OBJECTIVES OF THE UNIT

The Elizabeth Dafoe Library, one of 8 unit libraries and 6 satellite information centres within the University of Manitoba Libraries, supports the teaching and research requirements of the faculty and students of Arts, Education, Human Ecology, Nursing, Physical Education and Recreation Studies, and Social Work. Service is also provided to other members of the university community including off-campus students, and to the general public. The unit includes Circulation Services, Reference Services and the Icelandic Collection. The library contains over 830,000 books and bound periodicals; 430,000 government publications, 606,000 microforms; 100,000 maps; and subscribes to over 4,000 periodicals. Approximately 320,000 items are circulated each year. The Library performs the functions of access to collections, collection development, reference services, plus orientation and bibliographic instruction, and provides correspondence/off-campus library services.

The Off-Campus Library Services is the primary resource of students and faculty respectively enrolled in and teaching off-campus courses in all disciplines with the exception of Medicine, Dentistry, Dental Hygiene, and Medical Rehabilitation. Staff consists of 1 academic librarian, 1 library assistant and 1 part-time staff.

The incumbent reports to the Head of the Elizabeth Dafoe Library.

B. FUNCTIONS

1. To be responsible for the overall operation of the Off-Campus Library Services in all its aspects, including personnel management, planning and organization, and budget administration.

2. To develop and maintain an understanding of the off-campus programs and to plan and implement services in support of these programs.

3. To participate in the Libraries' policy-making decisions and development of services affecting off-campus students.

4. To provide traditional and virtual library services, including reference services, orientation and bibliographic instruction, and delivery of materials, and to serve as a liaison between the library user and the library system.

5. To develop and offer various modes of print and electronic instructional services.

6. To design and maintain a virtual library Web site which will include discipline-specific information resources and links to electronic resources and instructional materials.

.../2

Position Incumbent:
Position Title: Off-Campus Librarian
                        Reference Services Section, Elizabeth Dafoe Library
Page 2

7. To survey the needs with respect to library resources and services for off-campus students and to evaluate services on an on-going basis.

8. To promote the services available to off-campus students.

9. To evaluate and select materials for purchase in support of the off-campus programs and to manage the acquisitions funds allocated to off-campus library services.

10. To visit off-campus teaching sites in Winnipeg and rural Manitoba to evaluate the service and to provide instructional support.

11. To serve as the Libraries' liaison with Continuing Education and other faculties offering off-campus programs, thus ensuring communication and collaboration between the Libraries and the program providers.

12. In cooperation with the library units on the Fort Garry Campus and off-campus providers, to cultivate and maintain working partnerships with the community served and with community resources, i.e. community colleges, schools, public libraries.

C. EVALUATION CRITERIA

1. Effective management of the services.

2. Effective public relations and communication skills.

3. Ability to evaluate and meet the needs of patrons; effectiveness of

service to users.

4. Effectiveness of collection development.

5. Effectiveness of orientation and bibliographic instruction.

6. Ability to develop and maintain effective partnerships.

_____   _____
Incumbent   Date

_____   _____
Immediate Supervisor   Date

Washington State University
Position Description

Position Number: 38438
Appointment Status   Faculty, Tenure-track, Annual, 100% FTE
Organization and Location: Libraries, Pullman

Working Title: **Distance Learning Librarian**

Basic Function: Serves as library liaison to the Distance Degree Program (DDP); designs Web-based instructional resources and delivers instructional services to DDP students; participates in on-campus library instruction activities.

Reports to: Head of Library Instruction

Major Responsibilities

A. *Distance Degree Program Support* (50%)

1. Serves as liaison librarian for faculty and administrators in Distance Degree Programs.

2. Develops and manages the library Web sites that support DDP courses. Develops effective instructional materials using the Web and courseware like the Bridge and WebCT. Provides library instructional support for students enrolled in DDP classes.

3. Works with teaching faculty to develop effective research assignments for distance learners.

4. Coordinates library involvement with distance education consortia, WSU branch campuses and Learning Centers, and with other universities and community colleges.

5. Organizes, administers, and teaches General Education 300 for distance learners.

6. Supervises and directs temporary employees who assist with Web page development and maintenance.

B. Library Instruction (15%)
1. Teaches in the on-campus library instruction program and participates in library instruction
services, programs, and activities.

2. Collaborates with library instruction faculty and subject liaisons in developing Web-based instructional materials.

C. Reference Services (10%)
1. Provides reference service to library users at an on-campus reference service point using both traditional and online sources.

2. Participates in system-wide initiatives such as Digital Reference, as needed.

D. Collection development (5%)
1. Selects library materials in Russian language and literature.

E. Library and University Service (10%)
1. Serves on Libraries working groups, committees, and task forces.

2. Serves on university-wide committees and task forces.

F. Professional and Scholarly Activities (10%)
1. Keeps abreast of trends and developments in the fields of distance learning, library instruction, and related areas by reading professional literature, participating in professional associations, and attending workshops at the state, regional, and national levels.

2. Participates in research that may be shared and disseminated through presentation or publication.

3. Shares relevant information obtained from professional activities with library faculty and staff and uses knowledge gained to evaluate and improve library services.

Qualifications

REQUIRED:

HIGHLY DESIRED:

Signatures:

Title of Position   (Date)   Title of Supervisor
(Date)

This position description reflects Washington State University's best effort to describe the essential functions and qualifications of the position. This document is not intended to exclude an opportunity for modifications consistent with providing reasonable accommodation. This is not intended to be a contract. Your signature indicates you have read this position description and understand the essential functions and qualifications of the position.

Training Opportunities

UNIVERSITY OF MANITOBA

http://www.umanitoba.ca/uts/

UTS Home   Mission   Contact

university teaching services

Programs   Services   Resources   Publications   Awards

University Teaching Services (UTS) is a collegial faculty development program that initiates and organizes a wide range of activities related to teaching and learning. UTS programs are offered with the assistance of a growing number of University of Manitoba (U of M) faculty and visitors who work as consultants. The goal of UTS is to help enhance the quality of teaching and learning at the U of M.

Registration for the 2005 Spring Workshops now underway!

Spring Workshops Brochure (pdf)

Register online

Print out a pdf version of the registration form and mail or fax it to us.

News

March 2005 UTS Newsletter now available online (pdf)

Upcoming Events

New Faculty Workshop Series Registration Form

Teaching Techniques Workshop Series Registration Form

Subscribe to UTS' Listserv

UNIVERSITY of MANITOBA

UNL ❮ EE&O ❮ Faculty & Staff

UNL **Extended Education & Outreach**

84F/29c
SUNNY
61% RH
WIND SSW @ 8
as of 10:54am

EE&O Home | Programs | Students | Faculty & Staff | News | About Us | Conferences & Events

Extended Education & Outreach at the University of Nebraska-Lincoln

EE&O Quick Links ⬍ GO   search   EE&O Web ⬍ for   GO   🔍 ▦ 🔳 📷 ✂

Faculty and Staff Resources

The UNL Extended Education & Outreach program is dedicated to facilitating the offering of UNL's off-campus educational and outreach programs by assisting faculty in planning, designing and delivering distance courses and programs.

Here you will find information about planning and scheduling distance classes, delivery modes for distance courses, intellectual property rights, copyright laws, NU system and campus policies related to distance education, funding and grant programs and more. You can learn how to transform a traditional classroom course to an online format, review teaching strategies successfully used by other faculty and explore links to relevant information at other sites.

If at any time you have additional questions or find that you need assistance in planning, designing or delivering a distance education course or program, please contact us.

In addition to the wealth of faculty information, this site also contains information useful to the employees of Extended Education & Outreach. You'll find staff development ideas as well as helpful human resources links.

Welcome!
•
Request Additional Information
•
Contact Us

Faculty Resources

Frequently Asked Questions

Distance Education Policies and Standards

Distance Education Guiding Principles

Research and Grant Opportunities

Teaching Online
Introduction   Course Development

Planning and Scheduling

Instructional Design Support   *Delivery Options*

Training and Seminars   *How to Create an Online Course*

Copyright   *UNL Faculty Strategies*

Surveys and Results   *ID&D Blackboard Enhancement Tools*

Course Management

Topics in Distance Education

EE&O Staff Resources

Professional Development

Employee and Dependent Scholarship Information

Forms Directory

New UNL Employee Orientation

EULALIAGRASS

Cather Garden
City Campus

N © UNL | Office of Extended Education & Outreach | 900 North 21st Street | Lincoln, NE 68588-8500 | 402-472-2175 | comments?   *Pioneering new frontiers.*

PENNSYLVANIA STATE UNIVERSITY

https://courses.worldcampus.psu.edu/facdev101/student/index.shtml

**Welcome to the home page for
FAC DEV 101!**

Announcements

February 26, 2004 - Welcome to Fac Dev 101!

Welcome to Fac Dev 101, an online course designed for faculty who are new to the World Campus!

Fac Dev 101 will provide you with rich resources and important skills needed to develop and teach a distance education course effectively through the World Campus. In Fac Dev 101, you will have the opportunity to experience learning at a distance in a delivery environment which may be similar to the one you will use to author or instruct your own course. Lessons are constructed around competencies vital for all distance educators. To learn more about the course, please see the online course syllabus.

SELECTED RESOURCES

DOCUMENTS

Books, Reports, and Journal Articles

Barsun, Rita. "Walden University and Indiana University: Unlikely Partners Providing Services to Off-Campus Students." In *The Eighth Off-Campus Library Services Conference Proceedings,* compiled by Steven P. Thomas and Maryhelen W. Jones, 17–28. Mt. Pleasant, MI: Central Michigan University, 1998.

The author describes the efforts conducted between two universities to provide library services to distance students enrolled at Walden University. The paper is quite thorough in describing all the steps necessary to develop such a program, including the fostering of relationships with staff at both schools. The paper does not describe collaboration with faculty to develop instruction techniques; however, many of the issues discussed provide a springboard to those interested in developing better relationships with faculty for instruction programs.

Bell, Steven J. "Promotion through 'Teachnology.'" *Library Journal Net Connect* (Winter 2004): 15–16.

In this brief article, the author asserts librarians can resist marginalization by promoting low-threshold applications (LTAs) to their constituents. With mention of courseware products such as WebCT and Blackboard, the author proposes that the creation and management of content by faculty could lead to a further diminished library role. If, the author contends, libraries could market the library services with LTAs such as durable link e-reserves, direct interlibrary loan links, and alert services, among others, the library will maintain an active presence in teaching and learning environments. The author encourages the use of LTAs that are economical, can be documented on one page or less, and take little time to learn. He recommends the use of an archive of LTAs on the Teaching and Learning with Technology (TLT) Group Web site.

Buchanan, Lori E., DeAnne L. Luck, and Ted C. Jones. "Integrating Information Literacy into the Virtual University: A Course Model." *Library Trends* 51, no. 2 (Fall 2002): 144–66.

This article describes how librarians paired up with communications and composition faculty to team teach a distance learning course on multimedia literacy. The ACRL information literacy competency standards were written into the fabric of the course. Objectives were written to include the competencies and the learning outcomes based on those objectives were assessed. Some suggestions include creating Web pages specifically geared to distance education resources and services, inserting links to library resources within courseware, developing course-specific resource Web pages, using electronic portfolios, placing multimedia development suites or centers for academic excellence in the library, and creating Web-based instructional units. The team-taught course received mostly favorable reviews, though the information literacy component was not woven in with the media literacy content as much as it should have been. Rather, it was addressed at the beginning, almost in isolation. The teachers plan to work together again, but better integrate the content and stay on board through the entire course. It was also suggested that universities consider paying librarians on an overload basis for teaching as part of a team.

Buehler, Marianne A. "Where Is the Library in Course Management Software?" *Journal of Library Administration* 41, no. 1/2 (2004): 75–84.

Framed in the context of the environment at the Rochester Institute of Technology and specific courseware products, the author discusses the lack of a library component within the courseware and how this flaw necessitates creative librarian-faculty partnerships. The author advocates a central role by the library in the evaluation and selection process of campus-wide course management software.

Caspers, Jean, and Katy Lenn. "The Future of Collaboration between Librarians and Teaching Faculty." In *The Collaborative Imperative: Librarians and Faculty Working Together in the Information Universe,* edited by Dick Raspa and Dane Ward, 148–54. Chicago: Association of College & Research Libraries, 2000.

In this essay, the authors discuss the issues and trends of librarian and teaching faculty collaboration. The authors present the environment as one that is in a state of flux, particularly in reference to higher education institutions pressured to cut costs by using adjunct teaching faculty and how this trend has an impact on developing and maintaining librarian-faculty relationships. The essay continues by discussing the changing technologies and how they present challenges and opportunities for this collaboration, particularly in reference to distance education. The authors discuss the creation of a climate where the contributions of librarians to teaching and learning are recognized, expected, and valued by seeking collaborative opportunities constantly. In this collaboration, the authors conclude, the librarian will return to the scholar librarian specializing in a distinct body of literature with a more valued role and sought-after expertise.

Cassner, Mary, and Kate E. Adams. "A Survey of Distance Librarian-Administrators in ARL Libraries: An Overview of Library Resources and Services." *Journal of Library Administration* 41, no. 1/2 (2004): 85–96.

The authors conducted a survey of distance librarian-administrators in ARL member libraries. The 13-question survey concentrated on current distance education services, planned administrative and service modifications, budgetary concerns, and predicted trends. The majority of responses indicated library services are provided to distance education students and while services are expected to expand, budgets are not. Predicted trends included more collaboration among librarians, faculty, and other university partners; increased integration of library resources and services in course management software; and the creation of additional online and interactive library instruction materials. The survey questions are included.

Chakraborty, Mou, and Shelley Victor. "Do's and Don'ts of Simultaneous Instruction to On-Campus and Distance Students via Videoconferencing." *Journal of Library Administration* 41, no. 1/2 (2004): 97–112.

This practical article delineates the evolution of library instruction for distance students in a speech-language pathology course at Nova Southeastern University (NSU). The librarian taught the course via videoconferencing simultaneously to on-campus and off-campus students. She collaborated closely with the faculty member, expanding a one-shot bibliographic instruction (BI) session into a three-part class, based on the student feedback from previous classes. The transition from BI to information literacy was enhanced by incorporating graded assignments, student presentations, and quizzes. The authors present some of the challenges, recommendations, and solutions, and discuss the quality of teaching and learning comparing videoconferencing to face-to-face instruction.

"Characteristics of Programs of Information Literacy that Illustrate Best Practices: A Guideline." Chicago: American Library Association, 2005, http://www.ala.org/ala/acrl/acrlstandards/characteristics.htm (accessed July 1, 2005).

This ACRL document is intended for use by those developing, assessing, and improving information literacy programs. This list of characteristics of programs that illustrate best practices includes a section about collaboration among teaching faculty, librarians, and others.

Cooper, Rosemarie, Paula R. Dempsey, and Vanaja Menon. "Remote Library Users—Needs and Expectations." *Library Trends* 47, no. 1 (Summer 1998): 42–64.

This article presents a thorough review of literature regarding needs and expectations of both remote library users (people who choose to access the library resources/services remotely), and students enrolled in formal distance education programs. It correlates library user needs and expectations with those of other remote services: banking, e-commerce, etc. and includes data from a survey of students and faculty in a distance education course in nursing at DePaul University. While this article is very thorough in explaining issues of user needs and expectations, it has quickly become dated, e.g., the report from DePaul indicates that less than half of the students had Internet access.

Dawson, Alma, and Dana Watson. "A Marriage Made in Heaven or a Blind Date: Successful Library-Faculty Partnering in Distance Education." *Catholic Library World* 70, no. 1 (September 1999): 14–22.

The authors describe successful partnering strategies between librarians and faculty in distance education courses at the School of Library and Information Science at Louisiana State University. In addition to very practical suggestions for effective partnering, the paper includes a discussion of systems and systems theory as applied to the library services, education, etc. in the distance environment. The article also describes the skills and abilities librarians need to support effective distance learning and teaching.

Dewald, Nancy H., Ann Scholz-Crane, and Austin Booth. "Information Literacy at a Distance: Instructional Design Issues." *The Journal of Academic Librarianship* 26, no. 1 (January 2000): 33–34.

This article provides comprehensive coverage on how information literacy instruction must be modified for the distance education environment. Coverage includes information literacy instruction delivery options, examples of active learning methodologies, and assessment tools. The authors assert that technology, pedagogy, enhanced instruction design, and understanding of distant student learning behaviors must all be considered for effective information literacy instruction to distance learners.

Diercks-O'Brien, Gabi, and Ruth Sharrat. "Collaborative Multimedia Development Teams in Higher Education." *Educational Technology & Society* 5, no. 1 (2002): 81–85, http://www.ifets.info/journals/5_1/diercks.html (accessed July 1, 2005).

This paper describes the cultural issues that arise from multi-disciplinary collaborative teams. In 2001, the University of Sheffield funded several innovative information and communication technology projects as part of its learning media unit, a central multimedia development unit within the university. While there is no mention of libraries, it contains information that will be valuable to librarians who will be attempting to partner with academic units in the process of delivering distance learning information and/or instructional services. Production teams of all types need to develop appropriate models to work with academics who have differences in pedagogical approaches, and issues with curriculum development, ownership, leadership, and responsibility.

Dorner, Jennifer L., Susan E. Taylor, and Kay Hodson-Carlton. "Faculty-Librarian Collaboration for Nursing Information Literacy: A Tiered Approach." *Reference Services Review* 29, no. 2 (2001): 132–40.

This article explains how librarians at Ball State University became involved in curriculum development by working closely with nursing faculty members to create information literacy tutorials teaching targeted information literacy competencies. The tutorials were designed by librarians, while the exercises were designed by librarians and nurse educators working collaboratively. Each tutorial was preceded by a pretest, for evaluation purposes, and the modules were delivered via the Web, embedded in Web-enhanced nursing course modules at the point of need. The modules were distributed throughout each stage of the undergraduate nursing program in order to tie them to the courses and allow each instruction module to build on the one that came before. Librarians and faculty continued to collaborate after the course modules were completed, by regularly hosting chat room discussions with students. The article calls for librarians to move beyond one-shot library instruction and become involved in curriculum planning with faculty.

Edge, Sharon M. "Faculty-Librarian Collaboration in Online Course Development." In *Electronic Learning Communities: Issues and Practices*, edited by Sorel Reisman, John G. Flores, and Denzil Edge, 135-85. Greenwich, CT: Information Age, 2003.

This essay provides an account of librarian-faculty collaborative partnerships at the University of Louisville dating back to 1992. The author frames this account within a more general exploration of online course development, including sections entitled "Issues, Controversies, and Problems"; "Best Practices"; and "Future Trends, Emerging Technologies, and Research." The essay blends extensive research and a thoughtful analysis of a ten-year process of collaboration. Copious bibliographic references and several appendices outlining a variety of practical issues are included.

Feldheim, Mary Ann, Allison Ondrasik King, and Suzanne Sherman. "Faculty-Librarian Collaboration: Meeting the Information Technology Challenges of Distance Education." *Journal of Public Affairs Education* 10, no. 3 (July 2004): 233–46.

The collaboration among University of Central Florida librarians and distance education faculty members in public administration in the creation of an online research skills module is described in this article. An overview of the growth of distance education and the related required library services, followed by an overview of online resources available to public administration researchers are also provided. The authors give a detailed description of the creation, design challenges, and positive outcomes of the module created by faculty and librarians. Lessons learned by faculty, librarians, and graduate students are also included.

Fleming, Tim, William Tamone, and Michael Wahl. "E-Learning: Addressing the Challenges via Collaboration." ERIC, 2002. ED467854.

This paper presents a good case for increasing collaboration with other colleges to provide more online courses that give students the opportunity to complete a program from the Michigan Community College Virtual Learning Collaborative and not have to go elsewhere. Complete online programs include: criminal justice, network administration, and health insurance coding and billing. Facing academic challenges in developing online programs, classes, their delivery, and student support are discussed, such as a lack of fundamental resources.

Fletcher, Janet, and Des Stewart. "The Library: An Active Partner in Online Learning and Teaching." *Australian Academic & Research Libraries* 32, no. 3 (2001): 213–22.

Southern Cross University librarians discuss how they became active collaborators in building partnerships in their university's online learning and teaching development. Librarians' responsibilities have expanded to include more liaison activities and contribution to various online committees. The article contains practical applications for other academic settings.

Giles, Kara L. "Reflections on a Privilege: Becoming Part of the Course through a Collaboration on Blackboard." *C&RL News* 65, no. 5 (May 2004): 262–63, 268.

The author enthusiastically delineates her collaboration in a team-taught class with a history professor using Blackboard at a midwestern university. The librarian, in the role of a course builder, was able to become fully involved in the course. Having a direct rapport with the students, she was thereby able to help the students better with their research. The librarian's involvement in the Blackboard course received positive feedback. She also mentions her personal development as a librarian and some of the challenges of becoming a collaborator.

Gratch-Lindauer, Bonnie. "Comparing the Regional Accreditation Standards: Outcomes Assessment and Other Trends." *Journal of Academic Librarianship* 28, no. 1/2 (January/March 2002): 14–25.

This is a valuable article for libraries preparing for accreditation. The author delineates the new trends revealed in the documentation of the various regional accreditation commissions. She examines both their current standards and those in draft form, and determines that there is a much greater emphasis on outcomes assessment, distance education, and information literacy. The documents also advocate collaboration, innovation, and experimentation to improve teaching methods and increase student learning.

Guillot, Ladonna, and Beth Stahr. "A Tale of Two Campuses: Providing Virtual Reference to Distance Nursing Students." *Journal of Library Administration* 41, no. 1/2 (2004): 139–52.

The article describes the collaborative efforts of the health sciences and distance learning librarians with the faculty at the two campuses in Southeastern Louisiana University. In 2003 the librarians used a Virtual Reference Desk imparting bibliographic instruction to the distance nursing students using Tutor.com. The paper discusses this pilot program, detailing the initial collaboration, pitfalls and challenges, as well as the successes and considerations.

Heller-Ross, Holly. "Librarian and Faculty Partnerships for Distance Education." *MC Journal: The Journal of Academic Media Librarianship* 4, no. 1 (Summer 1996): 57–68, http://wings.buffalo.edu/publications/mcjrnl/v4n1/platt.html (accessed July 1, 2005).

The author discusses methods by which librarians and faculty cooperated in the creation of a new distance nursing program. Perhaps the area that benefited most from this collaboration was in the development of information resources to add value to the curriculum taught. The librarians went through a great deal of work to meet with the nursing faculty to discuss the curriculum and then regularly consult with faculty for input on how the library can better serve those associated with the new program. Based on the success of this collaboration the author suggests that the formation of partnerships can be carried over to all phases of developing new programs to both traditional and non-traditional students.

Hiscock, Jane, and Phillip Marriott. "Happy Partnership—Using an Information Portal to Integrate Information Literacy Skills into an Undergraduate Foundation Course." *Australian Academic & Research Libraries* 34, no. 1 (2003): 32–41.

At University of South Australia, undergraduates are required to graduate with specific attributes, called "foundations," which seem to correspond with general education requirements in U.S. schools. While there are four parts to the foundations, this article concentrates on the second of the graduate qualities, "lifelong learning in the pursuit of personal development and excellence in professional practice." Included in this quality are information literacy, computer, and communication skills. The course is called "Computer, Communication, and Society." There is a central portal for all four qualities which serves as a resources Web site and links all of the services that support the courses, in particular the library and student learning support centre. The authors, who are not librarians, emphasize the need for continuous communication and participation among the collaborators through the presentation of practicals (workshops) and regular communications about changes in resources and practice. The article illustrates some of the characteristics of collaborative activities: expertise or competencies in a variety of complementing and supportive areas among the participants, shared goals, and variety of communication venues and levels.

Ivey, Ruth. "Information Literacy: How Do Librarians and Academics Work in Partnership to Deliver Effective Learning Programs?" *Australian Academic & Research Libraries* 34, no. 2 (June 2003): 100–14.

The purpose of this very interesting article is to examine how collaboration between librarians and academics work. In the literature review, the author presents Shrage's 1990 list of elements for successful collaboration. She interviewed seven librarians and seven academics from three schools of study and compared the coded transcripts with the list of Shrage's list. She then ranked the items according to their apparent importance by the participants. Four of the behaviors were ranked as the highest (1) a shared understood goal; (2) mutual respect, tolerance and trust; (3) competence for the task at hand by each of the partners; and (4) ongoing communications. The author covers developing and sustaining respect, developing shared view of information literacy, negotiating teaching responsibilities, and planning a holistic curriculum. Major problems are due to the lack of resources, expressed in the academics' worry about the librarians' workload. One of the shortcomings of this study is its small survey size. The article contains an extensive library of references.

Kaufman, Frances G. "Collaborating to Create Customized Library Services for Distance Education Students." *Technical Services Quarterly* 21, no. 2 (2003): 51–62.

In the fall of 2001, Seton Hall University (NJ) tasked the client services librarian to expand library services to Seton Hall's distance education program. This case study demonstrates how collaboration between library liaisons and teaching departments led to customized Web pages and outreach services to distance education students. The article highlights planning process, review of the literature, and analysis of adult learners.

Kirk, Elizabeth E., and Andrea M. Bartelstein. "Libraries Close in on Distance Education." *Library Journal* 124, no. 6 (April 1999): 40–2.

This article provides a brief overview of several examples of librarians working to involve themselves in the development of distance education programs. It discusses promoting the library's role, as well as taking a proactive stance regarding instruction to serve distance learners, who have different learning styles from traditional students. In addition, this article includes a good list of online distance education resources.

Ladner, Betty, Donald Beagle, and James R. Steele. "Rethinking Online Instruction: From Content Transmission to Cognitive Immersion." *Reference & User Services Quarterly* 43, no. 4 (Summer 2004): 329–37.

The authors contend the pedagogical practice of cognitive immersion and the "classroom flip" in online course management systems necessitates the refocusing of library instruction from tool-based guides to technologies that foster greater interactive engagement practices and critical thinking skills. The "classroom flip" involves producing online lecture materials and using in-class (face-to-face or online) time for more involved discussion, student engagement, and active learning. The authors assert that embedded library instruction, collaboratively created with faculty, can further this kind of cognitive style immersion. An example project developed by nursing faculty and librarians is described.

Lockerby, Robin, Divina Lynch, Elizabeth Nelson, and James Sherman. "Collaboration and Information Literacy: Challenges of Meeting Standards When Working with Remote Faculty." *Journal of Library Administration* 41, no. 1/2 (2004): 243–53

The authors discuss the challenges and successes of collaborations with teaching faculty within the context of the National University Library Information Literacy Plan and the virtual Library Information Centers of National University. The core of the article is the report of three examples of successful collaboration in remote environments.

Markgraff, Jill S. "Collaboration between Distance Education Faculty and the Library: One Size Does Not Fit All." In *The Tenth Off-Campus Library Services Conference Proceedings,* edited by Patrick Mahoney, 451–64. Mt. Pleasant, MI: Central Michigan University, 2002.

The author acknowledges that collaboration between librarians and faculty needs to be fostered in order to effectively administer library instruction and services to distance students. Various methods to increase collaboration with faculty are discussed. These methods include conducting campus presentations and workshops, e-mail notices to faculty, and developing promotional and informational brochures. In addition, the author mentions the importance of including library support staff in the collaboration process.

OCLC E-Learning Task Force. "Libraries and the Enhancement of E-learning." Dublin, OH: OCLC, 2003, http://www.oclc.org/index/elearning/default.htm (accessed July 1, 2005).

This white paper comprehensively explains the dynamic and important relationship between libraries and the e-learning environment in higher education. The OCLC E-Learning Task Force, comprised of university librarians, instructional designers, administrators, and IT personnel, outlines the key elements in e-learning, including technology, pedagogy, learning methodologies, learning objects, metadata, repositories, and collaboration. The task force further explains how libraries relate to each of these elements and the higher education institution as a whole. In each section, the task force defines the challenges and opportunities libraries have in the e-learning infrastructure and how libraries can enhance their role, foster collaboration, and more successfully serve their clientele. Recommendations for libraries are included and the task force maintains that OCLC can take a leadership role in articulating library requirements and opportunities within the e-learning environment.

Ragan, Lawrence C. "Good Teaching Is Good Teaching: An Emerging Set of Guiding Principles and Practices for the Design and Development of Distance Education." *CAUSE/EFFECT* 22, no. 1 (1999): 20–24.

This article does a good job of drawing a framework for "guiding principles" in distance education. The principles are arranged in the following categories: (1) learning goals and content presentation; (2) interactions; (3) assessment and measurement; (4) instructional media and tools; and (5) learner support systems and services. Unfortunately, the article fails to include any mention of libraries or librarians. Nonetheless, the framework put forth could be useful in conceptualizing library support of distance education programs.

Riedel, Tom. "Added Value, Multiple Choices: Librarian/Faculty Collaboration in Online Course Development." *Journal of Library Administration* 37, no. 3/4 (2003): 477–87.

This article outlines collaboration at Regis University between teaching faculty, the distance education (DE) librarian, and instructional technologists. The concern for the librarian was how to make students aware of what is available in terms of distance education library services and resources, and how to use them for both online only and remote site courses. The main challenges included maintaining a librarian presence in planning and the limited faculty awareness of resources/services. The DE librarian worked with the Distance Education Unit within the School for Professional Studies to integrate library resources into online courseware (WebCT), essentially pointing to resources (including basic Web guides by subject) and still allowing them to be independently available through the library's Web site. The article details how the teams worked to implement different strategies for utilizing library resources in three different courses.

Rieger, Oya Y., Angela K. Horrie, and Ira Revels. "Linking Course Web Sites to Library Collections and Services." *The Journal of Academic Librarianship* 30, no. 3 (May 2004): 205–11.

A study was created to explore if and how library collections and services were integrated into course management software, CourseInfo, at Cornell University. After conducting a literature review and assessing the current usage of CourseInfo on campus, a sample of faculty using the courseware were surveyed. A key finding was that 45% of the faculty incorporate library resources in their CourseInfo site. E-reserves and databases were the most incorporated services. Not all faculty were aware of the usefulness of adding library resources to their sites and some faculty did not understand that off-campus users share the same access rights to library resources. The article includes an extensive list of recommendations such as continuing to use the course management software as an avenue for library services, the need for establishing a strong relationship with the university technology center, increasing the library's role in selecting and developing course management software on campus, encouraging increased collaboration among librarians and faculty when developing course sites, and developing more course-specific library tools that are easily integrated with the course sites. Other recommendations include investigating the viability of the university portal as another library service point, further developing personalized MyLibrary services, and possibly establishing a single user ID for CourseInfo and library resource access. As a result of the survey and subsequent recommendations, the Cornell University Library established a Personalized Library Services committee and a campus-wide Unified Services Working Group. A copy of the survey is included.

Rodman, Ruey L. "The S.A.G.E. Project: A Model for Library Support of Distance Education." *Internet Reference Services Quarterly* 6, no. 2 (2001): 45.

This article describes the process of creating a library resources and services Web page within WebCT for an online class at The Ohio State University. The author details the successful collaboration between the Health Sciences Library and a team of faculty in designing and delivering the Web-based instructional materials.

Sacchanand, Chutima. "Information Literacy Instruction to Distance Students in Higher Education: Librarians' Key Role." ERIC, 2002. ED472867.

This paper, from an IFLA conference, describes the changing state of the distance education environment, characteristics of distance students in higher education, and their problems in using library resources and services. The author discusses information literacy instruction as the key role of distance education librarians, based on a case study of Sukhothai Thammathirst Open University in Thailand.

Shannon, Amy W. "Integrating Library Resources into Online Instruction." In *Attracting, Educating, and Serving Remote Users Through the Web,* edited by Donnelyn Curtis, 171–95. New York: Neal-Schuman, 2002.

An applied, logical plan for integrating library resources into classes is presented. Suggestions are made as to how the librarian can establish credibility and a working relationship with faculty. Establishing interactive communication with the students is emphasized. Types of resources and ways to integrate them into the course are mentioned.

Stone, Virginia L., Rachel Bongiorno, and Patricia C. Hine Gardner. "Delivery of Web-Based Instruction Using Blackboard: A Collaborative Project." *Journal of the Medical Library Association* 92, no. 3 (July 2004): 375–77.

The collaborative creation of a Blackboard-based pharmacy tutorial is described including the review by the university's writing center, the placement of materials within the site, and the development of the voice-over for the Web pages. The tutorial has been made available to the entire campus and the results from an online survey indicate very favorable, campus-wide response.

Tillman, Mike. "Collaboration through Instruction Technology." In *The Collaborative Imperative: Librarians and Faculty Working Together in the Information Universe,* edited by Dick Raspa and Dane Ward, 60–4. Chicago: Association of College and Research Libraries, 2000.

The University of Washington received an endowment for an innovative technology initiative, called UWIRED, to facilitate teaching and learning in a networked environment highlighting communication, collaboration, and information technology. This case study describes this initiative tracing it back from its inception in 1994, and how the UW libraries came together under the UWIRED umbrella fostering collaborative projects between librarians and faculty. Initially, a selected group of students received laptops, as well as extensive information literacy and technology training. Laptops and "collaboratories"—a space adjacent to the library mixing a collaboration-friendly classroom and a computer lab—quickly caught the attention of the campus, state legislature, and the bibliographic instruction world. ACRL awarded UWIRED the Innovation BI Award. Evaluations showed that the UWIRED students fared much better than other students and the program was highly commended by faculty and students. Integrating technology into the curriculum allowed librarians to work closely with the faculty during the formative stages of instruction and librarians were available as on-site resources during the delivery of some innovative courses.

Ury, Connie Jo, Joyce A. Meldrem, and Carolyn V. Johnson. "Academic Library Outreach through Faculty Partnerships and Web-Based Research Aids." *Reference Librarian* 67 / 68 (1999): 243–56.

The authors describe the changes in roles and workloads of academic reference librarians at Northwest Missouri State University's Owens Library in response to the proliferation of online information resources. Based on statistics for questions answered at the reference desk, gate counts, and hits on particular Web pages, Owens Library reduced the desk hours of reference librarians and redirected that time to the development of Web-based, curriculum-centered research guides, tutorials, and bibliographies. They determined that to be the most efficient way to serve students, including distance-learning students.

Wright, Carol A. "Information Literacy within the General Education Program: Implications for Distance Education." *Journal of General Education* 49, no. 1 (2000): 23–33.

The author draws on experiences with the First Year Seminars at Pennsylvania State University and lessons learned from the libraries' participation in the Innovations in Distance Education project. Complexities in the new information and learning environments heighten challenges for providing user instruction and support, access to databases, and delivery of materials from a distance. The author affirms the role of information literacy as a critical component of successful undergraduate general education programs and argues that information literacy must be integrated with, not appended to, the curriculum. General education programs provide opportunities for librarians to develop strong partnerships with faculty.

Yang, Zheng Ye (Lan). "Distance Education Librarians in the U.S. ARL Libraries and Library Services Provided to Their Distance Learners." *The Journal of Academic Librarianship* 31, no. 2 (March 2005): 92–97.

In March 2004, the author conducted a telephone interview with 103 ARL member libraries to determine whether services are provided to distant learners, what services are provided, if a designated librarian is in charge of distance education services, and the concerns of those libraries with regard to distant library services. After a brief literature review and explanation of methodology, the author's findings include that more than half of the surveyed libraries provide services to distant education students, but only 21% have a librarian dedicated full-time to distance education services. Close to half of the distance education librarians report to the head of reference and more than half are involved in campus-wide distance education committees. Other findings suggest the library Web site is the primary distance education service point and a consistent, high use of document delivery and home-delivery of print materials. The survey respondents mention challenges such as the decentralization of distance education programs within the university and limited means for library service promotion among distance education students and faculty. Future studies are recommended; a copy of the survey is included.

SPEC KIT TITLE LIST

SPEC KIT PRICE INFORMATION (ISSN 0160 3582)

Subscription (6 issues per year; shipping included): $205 ARL members/$275 nonmembers (Additional postage may apply outside North America.)

Individual Kits: $35 ARL members/$45 nonmembers, plus shipping and handling.

Individual issues of the Transforming Libraries (TL) subseries: $28, plus shipping and handling.

SHIPPING & HANDLING

U.S.: UPS Ground delivery, $10 per publication.

Canada: UPS Ground delivery, $15 per publication

International and rush orders: Call or e-mail for quote.

PAYMENT INFORMATION

Make check or money order payable in U.S. funds to the ASSOCIATION OF RESEARCH LIBRARIES, Federal ID #52-0784198-N. MasterCard and Visa accepted.

SEND ORDERS TO: ARL Publications Distribution Center, P.O. Box 531, Annapolis Junction, MD 20701-0531
phone (301) 362-8196; fax (301) 206-9789; e-mail pubs@arl.org

ORDER ONLINE AT: http://www.arl.org/pubscat/index.html